# PROLOGUE

When I look in the mirror now I don't see the terrified child who was systematically abused, both mentally and physically. If you passed me in the street, you wouldn't notice either. You might see the small scar on my neck that was inflicted by a knife being pressed to my throat. You might notice a lump on my left wrist where the bones didn't heal properly after it was fractured. You might notice small scars on my arms where I was used as a live ashtray. But you won't see the scars that are deep inside me – the ones which take a lifetime to heal. They're ingrained in me, trapped under the surface like fish under a frozen lake, waiting for the moment when the surface cracks and they can come to life again. These mental scars are the demons that haunted me when I was at my lowest point. They came out to torment me, rearing their ugly head in the darkness. Then they would retreat again for a time, making me think I'd got over what happened to me, only to show up when I least expected it. But with every year that passed, I learnt how to handle the demons more. Every sick and twisted thing that happened in my childhood has made me into the woman I am today. I'm a survivor.

My name is Sarah and this is my story…

# Tell No One

## Sarah Cooper

# CHAPTER 1

My earliest memories are of living with my nan in Dorset. She had a small flat not far from Weymouth beach, and I would often spend my time staring out of the window at the sea, hoping I would spot Captain Pugwash. Nan always read stories to me before I went to bed and Captain Pugwash was one of my favourites. *One day I'm going to work on a boat and have great adventures just like him,* I thought.

Almost every day Nan would take me to the beach and help me build sandcastles. We'd spend hours there, getting them just right. My sandcastles had to be perfect, and we would scour the beach for stones or shells to decorate the turrets with so they looked like magical fairy castles. When Nan was too tired to carry on, she would doze in her deckchair while I built the moat and brought buckets of seawater to fill it up. I never got tired of the beach and often Nan would have to bribe me with a sticky bun or a fairy cake that she'd made, just so we could go home. On days when it was too wet or cold to venture out, I would play with a bright red plastic tea set that she'd given me. I'd put all my dolls out in a circle, spending hours imitating how Nan made tea and cakes, before we all sat down to a tea party of Nan's scones with thick butter and strawberry jam, washed down with a glass of milk.

Nan was a wonderful cook. She used to work in a canteen when she was younger, and she also had a fish and chip shop with my granddad who died a long time before I was born. Sometimes she'd let me help her make my favourite dish of Shepherd's Pie, and I'd stand at the kitchen table, pretending to chop up carrots like she did. Of course, she'd never let me have a proper knife, so I would just carve my plastic one against the carrot, making more mess than actually helping. But my favourite thing Nan made had to be the fairy cakes. She would put lots of chocolate chips in them, and my mouth watered as she cracked eggs into a bowl and added sugar, flour, and milk before pouring in a bag of chips. The best part was being rewarded by licking the bowl of raw, sweet mixture. I would dip my finger in again and again, running it along the sides and bottom, making sure I'd got every last drop. It tasted like pure heaven. Sometimes she'd decorate the cakes with icing and colourful hundreds and thousands that she told me were made from rainbows. She tried to get me to play while we waited for the cakes to cook but the smell was too much for me. Every few minutes I'd get up from the kitchen table, ignoring the drawing I was trying to concentrate on, and look into the clear glass door of the oven to see if they were ready.

'Are they ready yet?' I asked for the tenth time.

'They'll never be read if you keep watching them,' she chuckled to me. 'Come here.' She pulled me onto her lap and I snuggled into her warm neck, inhaling her Lily of the Valley perfume as she told me a story to take my mind off them.

Nan was quite plump and perfect for cuddling. I loved feeling her big arms around me, or resting my head on her soft chest as she often rocked me to sleep singing nursery rhymes. She always had endless amounts of cuddles for me

'I think the cakes are ready now,' she finally said after what seemed like an eternity.

I squirmed with delight on her knee before jumping off and following her to the oven. When she opened the door, I jumped up and down, waiting to get my first glimpse of them. After she put them on a cooling rack for a while, I was allowed to eat one when it was still warm, the chocolate chips inside still soft and melting in my mouth. Sometimes she would also make fudge, boiling up sugar, butter, milk, and vanilla extract that miraculously turned into the semi-hard sweet treats I adored.

Nan was also good at sewing. Having lived through the Second World War, she was able to make something pretty out of nothing. She had rolls of different off cuts of material and coloured spools of cotton that she kept in a wooden chest, and every time she thought I needed a new outfit, we'd look through the chest together to see if we had enough material to make a dress or a pair of trousers. At night I'd fall asleep on her knee to the constant clickety clack of her knitting needles making me a jumper, gloves, or a scarf.

I loved Nan so much and I wanted to live with her

forever, but she announced one day I'd be going to live with my mum again soon. I didn't remember my mum and dad. To me, they were just a photograph on the mantelpiece above the gas fire.

I knew that my dad had been in a car accident and was now with the angels and fairies, and that mum had taken it quite badly. I overheard Nan's other daughter, my aunty Linda, talking to Nan one day about mum's 'breakdown.' I didn't know what a breakdown was but they told me mum couldn't cope with me until she got better. Linda said mum had been in hospital for a while and was now on some kind of 'happy pills.' Soon she would take me to live with her.

Tears would well up in my eyes when they told me that I'd have to leave them. I loved Aunty Linda as much as Nan. She had two daughters, Beth who was five and Jane who was eight, and Linda always brought them to Nan's flat for us to play with each other, or I'd go and stay at Linda's to give Nan a much-needed break from looking after an active three-year-old. Linda's husband, Clive, had ginger hair and a red face from working outside all the time. He would throw me up in the air and catch me until his arms got tired, but I would always beg for more. On Sundays, Linda and Clive would take us all out for walks in the woods while Nan cooked a big roast dinner. As Beth, Jane, and I ran ahead, giggling, Clive would call us back and point out something shiny on the ground. We girls would run to this shiny thing, each trying to be the one to pick it up first. Whoever managed to grab it would gasp and then rush back to Clive with it twinkling in their outstretched hand.

A grin would pass between Clive and Linda as Clive said, 'It's a magical penny!'

'Why is it magic?' I said, handing it back to him.

'These pennies are owned by the fairies who live in the forest and they're hidden all over the place. If you find a penny, they'll protect you from the trolls,' he said, looking at us all in turn. 'Let's see how many you can find.'

Then it was a race as to who could find the most pennies and give them back to Clive. Little did we know that he was throwing the same penny on the ground all the time.

When I was about three and a half, I started nursery school. I was scared at first, hanging onto Nan's legs as we stood outside the small wooden hut on my first day. I sobbed uncontrollably, wondering why I had to leave Nan and play with the other children. As far as I was concerned, my life was already perfect so why did I have to go to nursery? But it didn't take long before I started to love playing with the other boys and girls. There were so many more toys than I had at Nan's. My favourite was a stuffed black cat that I called Dusty. As Nan left me at the nursery steps, I'd run inside to the toy box and claim Dusty for the day. I also enjoyed playing in the sandpit, painting pictures, or gluing glitter onto colourful pieces of card. When Nan picked me up at the end of the day, I would be covered in paint and glue with sand in my hair.

'Looks like I'll be doing more washing tonight.' She smiled and shook her head at me. 'How do you manage to get it everywhere?' She brushed the top

5

of my hair, sending grains of sand and glitter flying into the air.

I gave her a gappy-toothed grin. 'I don't know, but it's fun!'

The other children saw Nan waiting outside for me every day and asked me why my mum was so old.

'That's not my mum, that's my nan,' I replied.

'Where's your mum then?' they gasped.

I shrugged. 'I don't know. She's coming for me soon and I'm going to live with her.'

'What does your mum look like?'

I thought back to the photo on the mantelpiece. 'She's got long black hair and dark eyes with pretty green paint on them.'

'Where does she live?' they asked.

'In London.'

'When are you going to live with her?'

I just shrugged and ran off to play in the sandpit again.

One day, Linda came to pick me up from school and I knew something must be wrong.

'Where's Nan?' I asked.

She gave me tight smile and said, 'Your mum arrived today from London so she asked me to pick you up instead.'

I felt my stomach do a flip-flop, suddenly feeling uneasy.

'Does this mean I have to live with mummy now?' I scrunched up my face, ready to burst into tears at the thought of leaving Nan.

Linda bent down and hugged me towards her. 'It will be an exciting adventure for you.'

'But I don't want to go,' I wailed, throwing my arms around her neck and clinging on. I didn't even know the lady in the picture.

'Your Nan is getting older now and it's hard for her to look after you.' She patted my back and tried to calm me down. 'Besides, you belong with your mum.' There was something in her voice that I couldn't work out. She gave me a last pat and stood up, holding out her hand for me. 'Come on, let's go and meet her, shall we?'

I took a big sniff, wiping my nose on the sleeve of my jumper, and nodded meekly. If Nan and Linda thought it would be OK, then I didn't really have a choice.

My heart sunk down to my stomach as we walked the short distance home. Nan, Linda, Clive, Beth, and Jane were my world and the thought of leaving them was too much.

We stopped outside the door to Nan's flat and Linda smiled at me. 'We'll always be here for you. And we'll still see you lots. You can come and stay whenever you want. You'll like that, won't you?'

I glanced up and nodded slightly.

'And you might get to see the Queen in London,' she said, trying to make me feel better.

'Really? Will Captain Pugwash be with her?'

She laughed. 'Maybe.' She unlocked the door and led me inside.

The first thing out of the ordinary in the flat was the smell of cigarette smoke. I wrinkled up my nose and walked into the lounge with Linda's hand resting gently on my back.

Nan and Mum were sitting on the sofa, drinking

tea. Mum looked different to how she did in the photo. Her black hair was shorter, and instead of green paint on her eyelids, she had black lines drawn around them. Her lips were bright red and she had matching red long nails that reminded me of bird's claws.

Nan held out her hand to me. 'Come and meet your mum.' She smiled.

Mum put her mug of tea on the small table in front of her and smiled too, but it wasn't the warm kind of smile that Nan always gave me – the kind where her eyes twinkled. This was a cold smile, one that didn't reach her eyes at all.

I stood there, staring at Mum, unsure of what to do. Should I rush up and hug her like I always did with Nan?

'What have you been feeding her?' Mum turned to Nan. 'She's so fat,' she said with an undercurrent of aggression in her voice.

Nan kept her twinkling eyes on me but she sighed and I wondered if I'd done something wrong. 'She's a growing child. It's just puppy fat,' Nan said.

Mum beckoned me forward with a red talon. 'Come and give me a kiss then.'

Linda gave me a small push forwards and I walked towards her. When I was in reach, Mum pulled me closer and puckered her red lips so I could kiss her.

I kissed her mouth and was about to jump back again but she held my arms tight, studying me with narrowed dark blue eyes. 'God, she looks just like Geoff, doesn't she?'

Geoff was my dad who had gone to see the fairies.

Nan always said I looked like him. 'He was a lovely man,' she used to tell me. 'The salt of the earth. He'd do anything for anybody.'

But now, when Mum glared at me like that, it seemed like me resembling him was a bad thing.

Nan reached out to pat my head. 'Why don't you draw Mummy a nice picture, princess? Show her how good you are at art?' She nodded towards a pad of paper and my crayons in the corner of the room and I got to work, lying on my stomach on the lounge floor and drawing Captain Pugwash with Dusty and the Queen while trying to sneak glances at Mum.

Linda got a mug of tea and joined them on the sofa.

'So, how are you feeling?' Linda asked mum. 'Is everything...you know...back to normal?'

Mum laughed, a shrill sound. 'Of course. I'm on these new tablets and I feel fine now. I've even got a part time job in a café. And I'm getting married again!' She lit up a cigarette and inhaled deeply. 'I met Jim in the café I work in. He's a real gem.'

I glanced over and Mum showed Linda and Nan a glittery ring on her finger.

Nan's voice hardened. 'When's the wedding? And what about Sarah? She hasn't even met this Jim person.'

Mum waved a hand through the air casually. 'She'll meet him soon. That's why Sarah's going to come and live with us now, you see. Jim can help me cope with her.'

Linda stared into her tea and shook her head.

'What?' Mum snapped at her.

'You just leave her here for almost two years and then come back suddenly and announce you're getting married to someone she's never even met and she's coming to live with you. What sort of a mother, are you?' she whispered.

'I've been ill,' Mum spat.

'You were in the hospital for six months after Geoff died,' Linda said. 'That's a year and a half ago, but you didn't even phone Sarah or visit her in all this time.'

'It wasn't my fault. The doctor's couldn't get my medication right. Sometimes I couldn't even get out of bed. Anyway, I'm here now, and I'm going to make up for it,' Mum said brightly, tapping the cigarette into the ashtray.

'I hope so,' Nan muttered into her tea. 'What does this Jim do for a living?'

'He's a lorry driver so he's not really around much in the week but he's home every weekend.'

'When are you taking her?' Linda glanced over at me and caught me looking at them.

I quickly went back to my scribbling.

'Well, me and Jim are getting married next month so we thought we'd come and get her after that.' Mum's eyes lit up for the first time as she spoke about him. 'We'll be a proper family again.'

'Will you collect her before or after her birthday?' Nan asked.

Mum frowned. 'When's her birthday?'

Linda blew out a big sigh. 'You don't even know when your own child's birthday is?'

Mum giggled. 'Well, I know it's in May, of course. Twelfth? Thirteenth?'

'The sixteenth,' Nan said through clenched teeth. 'I'd like to give her a special party since it will be her last one here.'

'Don't be so dramatic.' Mum stubbed the cigarette out in an ashtray. 'It's not like you're never going to see her again. I can send her up here for holidays.' She stood up, smoothing down her tight black skirt. 'We'll come and get her the weekend after her birthday then.'

Nan stood up and walked towards me with a solemn smile. 'You mum's leaving now, princess. Give her the picture.'

'But it's not finished yet.' I stared at the picture that I'd only managed to draw Dusty in. I thought that somehow if I made the picture really good, Mum would like me, because so far she didn't really seem to.

'I'll get it next time,' Mum said, wandering over to have a look. 'What's that supposed to be?' She pointed to my efforts at drawing a cat.

'Dusty,' I said. 'She's my cat at nursery.'

Nan got to her feet and looked at the picture. 'It's lovely.'

Mum snorted at Nan, then said to me. 'So you like cats, do you?'

I nodded.

'Maybe I'll get you one as a special birthday present.'

My eyes lit up. 'What, a real one?'

She nodded, pulling me to my feet by one arm and squeezing me in tight hug, breathing her smoky breath over me.

'Wow, thanks, Mum.' Maybe living with her and

Jim wouldn't be as scary as I thought, especially if I had a cat of my very own.

Usually I'd be really excited about my birthday, but this year it meant that I'd be closer to leaving Nan and everyone else who loved me. I was worried about what to expect and started wetting the bed.

I would sleep straight through it and not even realise until Nan woke me up for nursery when I'd be devastated. This brought a fresh wave of anxiety as I wondered if Mum wouldn't love me because I couldn't control my bladder.

'Don't worry, princess,' Nan would reassure me. 'Most little children wet the bed.'

That made me feel a bit better, but I still nervously anticipated the day Mum and Jim would pick me up. I started to imagine that Jim was a jolly pirate like in Captain Pugwash and Mum was a nice princess who would look after me just like Nan did. I imagined they had lots of cats who would be my friends, which always seemed to cheer me up.

On the day of my fourth birthday, I woke up bubbling with excitement, wondering what presents I'd get. I pushed the crisp covers back from my bed and ran downstairs to the smell of fairy cakes cooking in the oven.

Nan prepared a special breakfast of boiled eggs and soldiers. The eggs had *Happy Birthday Princess* written on the shells, and she told me that a magic chicken had laid them especially for me. She handed me a present and I tore at the wrapping paper until it was just a heap on the floor. Inside was a stuffed black cat, just like Dusty.

I threw my arms around her waist. 'I love her. I'm going to call her Dusty.

Nan chuckled. 'I thought you might.'

Then we went to Aunty Linda's house and played games like pin the tail on the donkey, pass the parcel, and musical chairs, laughing until it was time for my birthday tea.

There were ham sandwiches, crisps, chocolate biscuits, Nan's delicious fairy cakes, and finally I was presented with a huge chocolate cake that had four candles on it.

'Don't forget to make a wish when you blow them out,' Linda said.

I couldn't decide what to wish for and kept everyone waiting. Finally, I decided to wish that everything would be OK with Mum and Jim, and I'd see Nan very soon. By the end of the day, the excitement was taking its toll and I was nodding off on the sofa. Geoff scooped me into his arms and put me in his car to take us back to Nan's.

As she tucked me into bed that night with Dusty firmly tucked under my arm, I thought it had been the best birthday ever. In the years to follow, it would remain so.

A few days later, Nan packed up my suitcase as I sat on the bed, sucking my thumb and cuddling Dusty with tears in my eyes.

'Now, now, don't cry. Everything's going to be OK.' She clicked the suitcase shut and gave me a warm hug.

'I'll speak to you on the phone, and your mum says you can come and stay with me too. We'll go to the beach, just like we've always done.'

A knock at the door interrupted us and Nan broke away. I noticed her eyes were wet as well.

'They're here,' she said, sniffing and wiping away the tears that had spilled down my cheeks. 'Come on now. I don't like to see my special little princess crying.'

Jim was a big bear of a man with blonde hair and bristles on the side of his face. He towered over me and I looked up at him, trying to stop my legs from shaking.

'So you're Sarah,' he said in a very deep voice, pinching my cheek hard.

'I'm dying for a cuppa, Mum, have you got the tea on?' Mum ignored me, looking up and giving Jim a glowing smile. I would come to recognise over the years that it was a smile just reserved for Jim – the only person who seemed to make her glow with happiness.

Mum she sat down on the sofa and lit up a cigarette.

'Aren't you going to give Sarah a kiss?' Nan frowned at her, shaking her head as she went off to boil the kettle.

Mum glanced at me as if she'd just noticed I was there and held out her arms.

I climbed onto her lap like I always did with Nan until she pushed me off.

'Stop wriggling. You'll get your dirty paws on my new skirt.'

I glanced at her under my fringe warily, sensing something new and scary was about to unfold in my happy life.

If Jim thought it was strange that Mum didn't

seem to have time for me, he didn't say anything. He just kept looking at his watch instead and saying, 'We'll need to make a move soon if we're going to miss the traffic.'

As soon as they'd drunk their tea it was time to say my goodbyes to Nan. From the back seat of the car, I watched her standing on the side of the road waving at me as tears steamed down my face.

As the landscape changed from wide open fields and farms to concrete buildings and housing estates, little did I know that my life was about to change forever.

# CHAPTER 2

I went from a loving, warm environment into a desolate world that confused me and taught me fear. Jim was hardly ever there, which meant I was with Mum most of the time, but she didn't seem to want me around.

She had no time to play or read me stories. She preferred to stay in bed, read her magazines, or watch TV. If I tried to kiss or cuddle her, she would push me off for one reason or another: I was messing up her hair or makeup, or I was making her clothes smell, since I wet the bed every night, were two of her favourite explanations. Gone were the days when I'd go to sleep with a bedtime story after Nan tucked me into the sheets. Now I had to put myself to bed at night. And when she discovered wet sheets again in the morning, she'd lose her temper.

'I'm not washing them every night. You can sleep in your own filth, you disgusting little brat!' Her eyes flashed with anger. 'I'm so ashamed of you. You're a disgrace.'

Sometimes I'd get a towel from the airing cupboard and place it over the dampness so I could get to sleep again the following night, hugging onto

Dusty and crying into his fur so that he too became damp. When she found a towel in my bed, she'd slap me around the head and lock me in the bedroom with no dinner and just a bucket to wee in. Sometimes I'd end up sleeping on the floor because the sheets were so damp and the urine started stinging my skin.

'If you can't use a toilet properly, you'll have to make do with a bucket. You're useless!' She narrowed her eyes at me in that now familiar stare, watching me cry and sniffle and say I was sorry over and over again.

'Good girls don't wet the bed. What did I do to deserve a child like you?' She slammed my bedroom door and I heard the turning of the key in the lock. Even now when I hear a lock clicking it sends shivers down my spine.

I thought that because I made Mum angry, I must be a bad girl and tried so hard to do everything she wanted me to and not make mistakes, but whatever I did never seemed to be right.

One morning she unlocked my door and shouted at me through the walls to get up for school. I was in a panic, trying to find a clean uniform, but I'd used them all up and she hadn't done any washing, so I rummaged around in the dirty washing pile and pulled on a skirt and blouse that still smelt of wee. I rarely seemed to have clean clothes because she would forget to take my clothes to the launderette. Somehow, she always managed to take hers and Jim's, though, and she always made sure she looked nice with new clothes that she bought for herself. I wandered into the kitchen to make my own

17

breakfast of cereal and milk because she would be too busy smoking and drinking tea or having a lie-in. As I poured Cornflakes into a bowl, she came up behind me, sniffing at my clothes.

'You smell like piss,' she yelled in my ear, making me drop the box of Cornflakes onto the dirty lino floor, spilling everywhere.

The next minute my head was bouncing off the wall as she roughly pushed me into it. I slumped to the ground in a state of shock and horror. I'd never been pushed or hit before and I froze in helpless panic. As she towered over me, I felt a gush of urine between my legs. I'd just done the very thing she'd been angry about and my heartbeat pumped hard as I wondered what my punishment would be.

'You filthy child. Have you no shame?' She yanked me by the arm, almost ripping my shoulder from its socket, and dumped me in the bath that had black mould in the corners.

She ran the cold tap as I sat there shivering with my teeth chattering uncontrollably, then she grabbed some rubber gloves from the cupboard under the sink and a bottle of bleach. She scrubbed me hard with a flannel until my skin started itching and burning. My cries seemed to spur her on even more so I quickly learnt not to shout out or shed tears because she revelled in my weakness, getting some kind of sadistic enjoyment from it, but when she pushed the flannel into my face, the bleach made my eyes water and burn and I couldn't help but yell for her to stop.

'Shut up.' She rubbed it harder into my face. 'If you want to be a dirty brat, this is what happens.'

18

'But Mummy it hurts!'

As my screams got louder she suddenly stopped. By then I couldn't open my eyes and they were streaming with water.

'Look what you made me do,' she shouted, turning on the cold tap again and hosing me down with the rubber shower attachment. 'It's all your fault. If you weren't so naughty, I wouldn't have to punish you. Why do you always do this to me?' She pried my eyelids open and ran the cold water into my eyes, which seemed to make them sting even more. I don't know if she finally realised that she'd gone too far, but the next minute she lifted me out of the bath and got me dried and dressed. 'Now I'll have to take you to the doctors and you'll make me late for work.' She dragged me down the road but I kept tripping and stumbling because I couldn't see where I was going. 'Don't you dare tell anyone about this,' she warned. 'If you tell anyone, I'll kill you.'

I knew she meant it. If she could burn my eyes and skin like that, she would definitely kill me if I said anything. And it must've been my fault. Mum always said that I should be punished for being naughty, but I wasn't sure what it was I did that made her cross all the time. I didn't want to do anything to set off her anger again so when the doctor asked me what happened, I kept quiet.

Sitting me on her knee in the doctor's office, she answered for me in a caring voice. I'd come to recognise now that Mum had two voices – a loving tone that she spoke to me in when there were other people around, and the angry, screeching tone that she reserved for me when we were at home alone. She seemed like a completely different person when we were in company; then she treated me like I was the best little girl in the whole world. She created a perfect illusion that seemed to fool everyone.

She gave the doctor a polite smile. 'You know what children are like, they're into everything. I turned my back for a second when she was in the bath and the next thing I knew, she was washing herself in bleach.' She stroked my head, giving the impression that she was a loving mother who hadn't just abused her child.

I wiped my streaming eyes again, trying to get a look at the doctor. Surely he'd know that she was lying, wouldn't he? He was a grown-up after all.

'Yes, they can be a handful sometimes.' He held my eyes open and shone a torch in them, then he put a couple of drops in each eye, which seemed to help with the pain. 'Maybe you should keep the bleach somewhere out of her reach from now on.'

'Of course, Doctor.' She smiled at him and he smiled back.

'I'm going to prescribe some drops for her eyes and cream for her skin. Bring her back in a week.' He handed her a prescription.

When we returned home, she made a cup of tea for herself and sat down, flopping forward and leaning on the kitchen table with her head in her hands.

'What did I do to deserve a child like you?' she moaned over and over again. 'Everything would be fine if I hadn't given birth to you. If I hadn't had you, my life would be happy. Do you know your dad was killed in that car accident on his way to visit you? Do you?' She lifted her head up and glared at me with accusing eyes. 'You killed him!'

I stood watching her with sore, blurry eyes, bewildered and unsure of what she wanted me to do or say. Was it really true? Had I made my dad die? I felt an emotion that I was too young to name – guilt.

Finally, she sat up and held open her arms to me.

Like a dog that's constantly kicked and bullied but still comes crawling back for more, I ran into them, desperately craving the love, affection, and approval that had been sorely lacking. I sat on her lap, snuggling in closer for comfort, hoping that she'd suddenly stopped hating me.

It wouldn't take long for her anger to surface again, though, and for the few cuddles she unexpectedly bestowed on me to cease completely, and I soon learnt not to trust her.

It was better at the weekends when Jim was home from work because she couldn't do as much to me without him noticing. During the week, he slept in lorry parks as he drove up and down the country delivering goods, but every Friday night he'd come back to the flat in London. Whenever he was around, she'd act like a completely different person. She smiled and giggled a lot and spent more time in her bedroom with him. Although he, too, ignored me a lot of the time, at least he was usually kind and often bought me presents.

I was playing with a new doll that he'd brought back with him one weekend when Mum announced we were going to the park to feed the ducks.

She got all dressed up in her new clothes and fur

coat, and even helped me get dressed into some new jeans that Jim had bought me. For the first time since I'd arrived, she brushed my long hair, getting out all the knots that had formed during the week because I forgot to brush it every day. I think Jim must've noticed that I was always dressed in inappropriate clothing because Mum hardly ever did my washing and never bought me anything new to wear. In winter I would shiver in thin cotton T-shirts and skirts with no tights, and in summer I'd be wearing thick polo-necked jumpers and jeans because they seemed to be the only clean clothes to wear. Sometimes Jim would bring me some new item of clothing back at the weekend and he would want to see me wearing them. Those were the few times I actually got to wear clean clothes.

For a moment the old familiar longing came back that Mum was going to start being nice to me, loving me like Nan used to, but just after she finished brushing my hair, she dug her fingernails into the tops of my bare arms and said, 'Don't you dare do or say anything to show me up. If you make Jim angry, he'll leave me, and no one will want a woman with a brat.' Her fingernails pressed tighter, drawing blood. 'Do you understand? I've given up quite enough for you already. I'm *not* giving up Jim.'

I nodded silently, trying to stop my eyes from watering because that would just encourage her to do it harder.

'Don't forget the bread for the ducks.' Jim grinned at me before we left the house.

'Sorry!' I rushed into the kitchen to get half a

sliced loaf that was left from earlier in the week and was green with mould. After the incident where I spilled Cornflakes on the floor, Mum told me that I couldn't have breakfast anymore because I'd made such a mess. She counted all the slices of bread and things in the fridge so I couldn't even take something to eat without her noticing or I'd get another beating. Lately, she'd started kicking me in the stomach or legs too, leaving big, painful bruises on my skin. I stared at the bread, my stomach rumbling with hunger, wishing I could sneak a few mouthfuls before she realised. Then I came to my senses. It wouldn't be worth living if she thought I'd taken some food without her permission. Once before, I'd come home from school and she'd accused me of taking a packet of crisps out of the cupboard.

'Did I give you permission to have a packet of crisps?' She glared at me as I slunk into the kitchen while she was peeling potatoes in a sink full of water.

My eyes widened in surprise. I didn't have a clue what she was talking about.

'I didn't take any crisps,' I said, backing out the door away from her.

She put the potato peeler down on the draining board with a loud bang and swung around to face me. 'Really? Well why is there one packet missing then?'

I shook my head. 'I don't know.'

'I don't believe you. You're a liar, aren't you?'

I shook my head. 'I really haven't taken them, honestly.'

'No body likes a liar.' She beckoned me towards her. 'Come here.'

I did as I was told, taking tentative steps in her direction.

She grabbed my hair and pushed my head down into the cold water in the sink, holding it under the water so I couldn't get up.

My arms flailed around behind me as I panicked, but she continued pushing on the back of my head with such force that I thought I'd drown.

Finally, she pulled my head back up by my hair and I gasped for breath.

She slapped me around the head a few times. 'Don't even think about stealing from me again.'

After that incident there was no way I would dare to sneak some extra food, even if she wasn't looking. Somehow, she had an all-seeing eye and would know if something was missing.

'Come on,' Mum called impatiently from the hallway. 'Don't keep Jim waiting. The ducks will be gone if we don't hurry up.'

I hurriedly grabbed the bread and darted off to join them.

As we walked along the street I heard Jim saying to Mum, 'Is she eating properly? She looks like she's losing a lot of weight.'

'She needs to, the fat little lump.' Mum laughed. 'Sometimes she refuses to eat what I cook her. I can't force her to eat, can I? You know what kids are like. They're so fussy.'

This was an absolute lie, but I didn't dare say anything in case it ignited her temper again when Jim wasn't there, or in case he left her and she blamed me. At weekends, Mum cooked nice dinners for herself and Jim but during the week Mum would cook her own dinner and just give me leftover scraps. Occasionally, she'd make me a sandwich for my evening meal or heat a tin of spaghetti hoops, but the more I asked her for food, the more she ignored me or gave me a slap or a kick, so I learnt not to say anything at all. I'd long since forgotten what Nan's delicious home-cooked meals tasted like. Luckily, at school they always gave out a pint of milk for morning break, and because we were a low income family I had free school dinners so at least I got a hot meal for lunch, even if it was sometimes revolting things like cabbage or stew, and blancmange or semolina for pudding.

'Stop worrying about her.' Mum linked her arm through Jim's and smiled like she didn't have a care in the world. 'She's fine.' She turned to me and held out her hand. 'Come here, Sarah, and tell Jim how you don't like Mummy's cooking.'

Nervously I watched her, wondering what she'd do next.

She beckoned me towards her, giving me a glare that Jim didn't see. 'Come on. Come to Mummy.'

I got closer to her and held her hand.

She squeezed it so hard I thought she might break my fingers, her nails digging into my skin in a silent warning. 'Tell Jim how you're such a fussy eater.'

I made up some story about how I was so full up after the lovely school dinners that I couldn't eat the tea that Mum made for me.

'See?' She grinned at Jim. 'She's such a one.' She

carried on squeezing my fingers.

When Jim left that weekend, she stamped on the doll he'd recently given me and told him I'd lost it at school. No matter how many times she was nice to me in public, she would show her true side when we were on her own and the abuse would continue unchallenged. Even though I was still so young, her terror was already escalating.

# CHAPTER 3

My sixth birthday arrived without even a card or a 'Happy Birthday' from Mum. Nan and Linda called to speak to me in the morning but, as usual, they were told that I couldn't talk to them because I was out playing with my friends. I was forced to listen to Mum telling them stories about how happy I was and how I was doing brilliantly at school as she gave me the familiar stare that told me to keep quiet or my life wouldn't be worth living. I longed to be Nan's little princess again and play with her and Linda and my cousins. I missed them terribly and wanted to feel their arms around me, telling me everything would be all right, instead of feeling the pain and hatred every day. Mum's promise that I could stay with Nan during the holidays never materialised either so I hadn't seen her or Linda for two years. I'd often cry myself to sleep thinking about them and wondering if they missed me as much as I missed them.

Even though I couldn't see Nan and Linda, it didn't stop them from sending birthday presents to Mum's flat, but I wasn't allowed to open them.

I was getting ready for school in another dirty uniform when Mum came into my bedroom and said, 'Come into the kitchen, brat, and let's see what they got you for your birthday.' She had a wicked smile on her face and I stopped unbuttoning up my blouse, feeling pure dread. Sometimes I even forgot that my name was Sarah now, since she only ever called me Brat, Fatty, Useless, or Ugly. The only time I ever got called Sarah anymore was when Jim was around or when I was at school.

My knees shook as I wondered what to expect. Seeing as it was my birthday, would she be nice to me? Or would the nasty Mum that I knew so well still be there?

She puffed on a cigarette, staring through the hazy smoke at my shaking hands.

'What's the matter? Anyone would think you were scared of me,' she said in a chilling voice. 'Are you scared of me?'

I didn't know what the right answer was. I was petrified of her, but if I said yes, it might not be what she wanted to hear and she'd punish me. If I said no, she might think she wasn't punishing me enough. I could never win, and most of the time I didn't dare answer her for fear of setting her off again.

I squeezed my legs together so I wouldn't wet myself out of sheer terror.

'Answer me!' she screamed.

I nodded my head mutely.

A smile of satisfaction formed on her lips before she ripped open the colourful wrapping paper on Nan's present.

I craned my neck to get a better look at what Nan had bought me, but I didn't venture within striking distance of Mum.

'Well, isn't that nice?' She held up a couple of comics to show me, then slapped them hard down on the kitchen table, making me jump in fear. 'What else have we got?' She took her time drawing on her cigarette before blowing it out in my direction, causing me to cough and splutter. After an interminable wait, she stubbed it out in the overflowing ashtray and opened the next present. A box of beautiful colouring pencils in a shiny tin.

I gasped with delight. Nan always encouraged me to draw, saying that everything I did looked like a colourful masterpiece. Now I drew to lose myself in a world that I could make up – one where I was still a beautiful princess and had a knight in shining armour to come and save me on a galloping white horse.

Mum narrowed her eyes at me and opened the next one. It was a box of Nan's fairy cakes.

I eyed them hungrily but didn't say anything.

Mum held one up towards me. 'I bet you want to eat one of these before school, don't you?'

I nodded, my mouth watering.

'Well, what do you say then?'

I reached out to take it. 'Please can I have one, Mummy?'

She snatched her hand away and ate it in front of me. 'Mmmm.' She licked her fingers leisurely one by one. 'What?' she said in a mocking tone. 'Are you hungry? Did you want one?'

I'd got used to the daily hunger pains in my stomach by now but the thought of Nan's fairy cakes was too much to bear and I let my guard down.

'Yes. Please can I have one?'

'They're so tasty. I'm not surprised you want one.' She closed the lid of the box. 'Maybe if you're good you can have one when you get home. But seeing as you're so hungry now, I've got something else for you to eat.' She pushed the ashtray towards me.

I didn't understand what she meant at first, but then it became all too clear.

'Eat the butts.' She leant back in her chair and folded her arms.

'But I don't want to.' The thought made me gag already. I hated her stinky cigarettes. 'People aren't supposed to eat them. Please don't make me.' I looked at her, horrified.

She laughed at my obvious distress. 'Which people aren't supposed to eat them?'

'What do you mean?' I asked, my knees shaking, afraid I'd get another punishment if I didn't do as she asked.

'You said people aren't supposed to eat them. Are you saying grown-ups aren't supposed to eat them?'

'Yes.'

'What about pathetic little brats who are naughty?'

'They're not supposed to eat them, either.'

'Who says?'

'I…I don't…know,' I stammered, confused about what she wanted me to say.

She tapped her long fingers on the table. 'Come on! Tell me!' She shouted. 'Who says little brats aren't supposed to eat them?'

'I don't know,' I wailed, staring at the cigarette butts and willing them to disappear in a puff of smoke.

'Well, I say that children *do* eat them.' She glared at me. 'So are you calling me a liar?'

I shook my head. 'N…no.'

'Good. You want to be a good girl on your birthday, don't you?' Her eyes narrowed.

I wiped my tears away with the heel of my hand. 'Yes,' I whispered, backing away into the corner of the room and cowering.

'If you do as you're told and eat them, then you can have some fairy cakes when you get home from school. Cakes are only for *good* girls.' She picked up one of the butts and shoved it in my hand. 'What are you waiting for? Go on! Eat it before I get really angry and it'll be even worse for you.'

I put it to my mouth with shaky fingers but the smell was overpowering so I lowered it again, looking at her for some kind of last reprieve.

'Eat it,' she said calmly, which was even more frightening than if she was yelling at me.

I held my nose and put it in my mouth, chewing and chewing as quickly as I could but I couldn't break down the filter. The taste and consistency in my mouth made me retch, and I vomited all over the kitchen floor.

She leapt out of the chair and pushed my head down into the vomit, rubbing my nose in it. 'Look what you've gone and done now, brat! Eat it up.'

The smell made me gag even more and I threw up a fresh wave of vomit.

She pushed my face so hard into it that I couldn't

breathe. 'Eat it.'

Sweat poured off my forehead as I kicked my legs and struggled to get away but she sat down on top of me so I couldn't move and could barely breathe.

'Lick it all up like a good girl,' she ordered. 'You want to please me, don't you? You want to be a good girl for once.'

I clenched my eyes shut and licked the floor as quickly as I could before I brought up anymore.

When she thought I'd had enough I felt her weight lift off me and she said, 'Now go and get cleaned up for school. You filthy little brat, you stink.'

I rushed to the bathroom and was sick again, flushing the toilet so she wouldn't make me lick that, too. With eyes blurred from so many tears, I stripped off my uniform and found another one that, while it was still grubby, didn't have any sick on it.

'Now get out of my sight. I'm sick of looking at you,' Mum yelled as I tried to brush the vomit out of my hair. She grabbed me roughly by the arm and pushed me out of the door, and I could feel her eyes burning a hole in my back before she slammed it shut.

I was still trembling as I walked the half an hour to school. What did I do to make me such a bad girl? Why didn't my mum want me? Was it normal for a mum to act like this?

Although part of me liked being at school because it was the only time I could get away from her, the other part of me was still unhappy there. Because I was dirty and unkempt and often smelt, the other kids would avoid me or call me names. In assembly there was a noticeable gap around me as we all sat on the floor, and I would feel just as unloved and abandoned there too. I was shy and retreated even more into myself to avoid yet more taunting and bullying from the other kids, burying my head in a book instead.

At one time I did get quite friendly with a girl in my class called Lisa, and whenever she invited me over to her house after school for tea, I would always have to say no. Mum told me that she didn't want me making friends with any of the local kids because they were no good. I think it was just to make sure I didn't tell anyone's parents what was happening at home. She constantly drummed into me that she would kill me if I ever told anyone what she did, and even I did tell, she said no one would believe me. Her act of being a loving mum in front of everyone must've fooled them all. I was too scared to ask a teacher or a parent if my life was normal, so I lived in a secret world of terror, too afraid to speak up in case I got an even worse beating or she did actually kill me. In the beginning she was always careful not to leave marks on my face so I could cover up the bruises and cuts with clothes. If I had gym class, she would make me wear long trousers and long sleeved tops so no one could see the scars she inflicted.

Because I wasn't allowed to hang around with Lisa after school and at weekends, it wasn't long before she started ignoring me, too, and I lost the one person who might've actually been a friend to me.

When I turned up at school on that birthday, I must've looked upset because my teacher asked me to go with her to the library while the other kids did a writing exercise.

She sat me down in one of the small chairs and perched on a table opposite. 'Are you OK, Sarah?' She rested her hand gently on my shoulder.

I nodded silently, willing myself not to cry, but the kindness in her eyes seemed to make me feel worse.

'Is everything all right at home?' she asked softly.

I wanted to scream that my mummy was horrible to me. That she beat me, taunted me, starved me. I wanted to cry out that I was afraid all the time, but I didn't make a sound. I had to keep it all inside in case Mum found out I'd told someone.

'Sarah?' she prompted me again. 'It's OK, you can tell me.'

I took a deep breath. 'Everything's fine, miss,' I lied.

'OK. Well, if you ever want to talk to me, you can.' She smiled, then squeezed my hand and said, 'It's your birthday today, isn't it?'

'Yes,' I whispered.

'There will be a special birthday surprise for you at lunchtime.'

My eyes lit up. 'A special surprise? Just for me?'

She nodded and stood up, holding out her hand. 'Now come on, the quicker we get back to class, the quicker lunchtime will come around.' She winked at me.

I spent all morning wondering what the surprise would be. Would Nan or Linda turn up to take me back to live with them? Would it be a nice present from the teacher? And if it was, how could I get it

34

home without mummy noticing and destroying it?

Lunchtime seemed to take an eternity to arrive and I fidgeted eagerly in my seat. When our class was called into the dining room I sat down, glancing around with excitement to see if I could see what the present was. I wolfed down my food, as usual, but when they served the pudding and then everyone rushed outside to play, I realised that there was no surprise.

I sat in the furthest corner of the playground like I always did, trying to become invisible so I wouldn't be subjected to name calling. I watched the other kids playing kiss chase and hopscotch and wondered what I'd done to deserve my life.

I was the first one back in the classroom after lunch. As the bell went, all the other kids ran in noisily and sat down. When our teacher arrived, she called me up to the front of the class and I had to sit there, blushing, while the other kids looked on. I waited nervously, wondering what I'd done wrong now and what kind of punishment I'd get. I squirmed with embarrassment as the other kids whispered to each other about me and pulled faces that the teacher couldn't see. Tears pricked at my eyelids. All I wanted was a normal birthday where I would feel loved and protected, and yet even at school I must've been a naughty girl because the teacher was going to punish me for something too.

She told everyone to wait and be quiet and she slipped out of the room. When she returned she was carrying a huge birthday cake with white icing and six lit candles on it.

My jaw dropped open. All this cake for me? How

lucky I felt at that moment.

'Surprise!' the teacher said, putting the cake down on her desk carefully. She grinned at me. 'Do you want to make a wish?'

I jumped off the chair and rushed to the desk. What should I wish for? I stood there for ages, trying to think. There were lots of things I wanted. To be living with Nan again. To make Mum love me so she wouldn't be horrible. To make the violence stop. To be cuddled and kissed again. To feel loved.

I blew the candles out and wished that Nan would come and get me soon, then I launched myself at the teacher and hugged her legs tight. This would probably be the only birthday present I'd be allowed if Mum had anything to do with it.

The teacher laughed and crouched down in front of me. 'Happy Birthday, Sarah.' She gave me a kiss on the forehead – the first kiss I'd had since I'd left Nan. Then she made the whole class sing Happy Birthday to me and got some paper plates and a knife from her desk, cutting the cake into twenty small pieces. It was my job to hand around a slice to all of my classmates. I got an extra big piece. I'd forgotten what cakes tasted like and it was so delicious. That afternoon even the other kids were nice to me for a while, but as soon as it was time to go home all the familiar feelings of dread returned as I wondered what new tortures Mum had thought up during the day. When I got home Mum was asleep. I hunted around the house for my presents from Nan and Linda and found them in the bin. The comics had been ripped to shreds, the pencils had been broken into pieces, and the fairy cakes had cigarettes stubbed out in them. How had my happy life unravelled so quickly?

Happy Birthday, Sarah.

# CHAPTER 4

A little while after that birthday, Nan came for a surprise visit. I came home one day from school and she was sitting with Mum at the kitchen table. A box of her fabulous fairy cakes were open next to their mugs of tea.

I rushed into Nan's arms, feeling her envelop me in a soft, squishy hug and shower me with kisses.

She pulled back, studying me carefully with a huge smile on her face. 'What happened to my little princess? You're such a skinny little thing.' She stroked my hair, which she used to brush for hours and put in pigtails and ponytails. Now it was always matted, dirty, and lifeless. 'And what's happened to your hair?' She glanced over at Mum and glared at her. 'What are you doing to this child?'

I was instantly ashamed that Nan had seen me looking like a dirty little girl instead of the squeaky clean child she used to bath every night. Mum ignored her and lit up a cigarette. She got up and grabbed a bottle of brandy from the cupboard and poured a hefty slug into her tea. I'd often seen her do this lately. Even in the mornings she'd put brandy in her tea.

Nan looked at her watch, tutting. 'It's half-past

four. Why are you drinking at this time? Are you supposed to drink with your medication?'

Mum waved a dismissive hand. 'It's just a small tot. I'm off the medication now and I feel fine.'

I sat on Nan's knee as she handed me a fairy cake. 'You need fattening up, princess. Have one of these.'

I munched away as Mum gave me her signature narrow-eyed stare, daring me to say something bad about her. When I finished eating the cake, Nan rummaged around in her big bag and handed me a new stuffed cat.

'I thought your old Dusty would be getting a bit tired by now so I brought you a new one.' Nan smiled.

I threw my arms around her neck, breathing in Lily of the Valley perfume. Since Dusty was now old and falling apart and smelt of wee, this new toy was the most welcomed present.

Nan told me to go and play in my bedroom while she talked to Mum. I didn't want to be parted for a minute from Nan but I did as I was told so as not to spark off Mum's wrath when Nan left. After a while, I heard raised voices in the kitchen.

'You're not treating her properly,' Nan said. 'Look at the state of her!'

'She's such a wilful and naughty brat; you don't know what it's like. If I tell her to do something, she refuses.'

'Why does she look so filthy? Aren't you doing any washing? And what are you feeding her? She's lost so much weight.'

'I feed her perfectly fine,' Mum's voice rose. 'She

doesn't like what I cook her and just picks at her food. All kids are like that.'

Nan sighed loudly. 'Isn't Jim helping you?'

'He's at work all week, what do you expect him to do?' Mum snapped.

'I think you need to go and see the doctor again and get some more tablets. It's obvious you can't cope with a small child.'

'I'm fine. I don't need anything. I think I know what's best for my own daughter.'

'Why don't you let her come and stay with me for a while?' Nan asked.

A bubble of excitement welled up inside me. Stay with Nan? Could I? Would Mum really let me?

'Why would you want her?' Mum said. 'She'd just get under your feet. Besides, me and Jim would miss her. Her place is with here with me. I'm not working anymore so I've got lots of time to spend with her.'

Nan pleaded with her to let me come and stay but Mum kept refusing. In the end, Nan gave up asking her and took me out to the park to feed the ducks. She asked me lots of questions about what it was like living with Mum, but what could I say? I wanted to tell her everything but I knew if Mum found out, it would be all the worse for me, so I lied and said it was great. I hated lying to Nan, and I hated Mum for making me lie. Nan bought me an ice cream and as we headed back home to that hellhole, I had tears in my eyes. I clung to Nan's legs before she left to get the train back to Dorset. I wanted to cry out to her what was really going on, but my screams were locked inside my throat.

'Be a good little princess for me.' She hugged me. 'I'll come and visit you again soon.'

That was the last time I saw her.

After she left Mum took great pleasure in seeing my tears and taunted me, hand on hip, glaring. 'Oh, so you want to go and live with your Nan, do you? What's the matter, brat, aren't I good enough to live with?'

I stared at my feet, not daring to make a sound.

'Well? Aren't you going to answer me?'

The next minute she dragged me by the hair so hard that my scalp felt like it was on fire. She pulled me into the lounge, screaming furiously so that spit was flying out of her mouth and landing on my face, and calling me every name she could think of. 'Don't think you can go behind my back and call your Nan. You stupid cry-baby brat.'

'I didn't call her,' I whimpered.

'Why else would she come and visit?' she sneered. 'I bet you've been using the phone when I've been asleep to call her. You stupid cry-baby.'

'I didn't phone her, honestly,' I pleaded.

'Stand over there.' She growled, pointing to the corner of the room.

Shaking, I went to stand in the corner, wondering what she would do next.

She grabbed a heavy encyclopaedia from the bookshelf and crashed it down on my head so hard that I saw stars. I slid to the floor, but she yanked me up by my arm.

'I said, stand there! You're not going anywhere until I say so.' She forced my arms above my head and thrust the encyclopaedia in my hands. 'Now stay like that until I tell you otherwise.'

She left me standing there holding the heavy book above my head and disappeared for a moment. When she came back in the room she had a mug of tea that smelt like brandy and a cigarette in her mouth. Sitting down on the sofa, she flicked lazily through a magazine, looking up every now and then to make sure I was still holding the book.

As my arms began to wobble uncontrollably and I felt the room swaying with dizziness, I started whimpering. The pain was getting too much, and I knew that pretty soon I'd have to put the book down, but then the punishment would be much worse. I had a headache so bad it felt like my brain was going to explode and my stomach churned.

'Don't even think of putting it down until I say.' She glanced up. 'I bet it really hurts your arms, doesn't it?' She looked very pleased about this, excited. 'Well now you know what it feels like! God knows, you've hurt me enough.' She went back to her magazine.

I wasn't sure what she meant. I'd never done anything to hurt her.

My arms dropped lower and lower until I was resting the book on my head. I don't know what happened next because I passed out, weak from hunger and fatigue. When I woke up I was lying on the floor of the lounge and the flat was in darkness. Mum had obviously got fed up with witnessing her torment and gone to bed. For that, I was grateful for. It could've ended up much worse.

Not long after that incident it was Mother's Day and at school the teacher happily announced that we would be spending the morning creating a Mother's Day card. I thought that if mine was really good it would show Mum that I wasn't such as naughty, disgusting child as she thought, and if the card was extra special maybe she would start to like me. We could choose different colour paper to use for the card and I chose red because it was the colour Mum always used to paint her nails and lips with so I thought it must be her favourite. I spent hours carefully trying to draw pretty flowers and birds, covering them with sparkly glitter. I even drew a picture of Mum and me. She was holding my hand and smiling a big smile, something I hardly ever saw in real life. I was smiling in the picture too, which had now become another rare occasion.

I sat back at the end of the lesson, pleased that my card was as good as it could possibly be, and with excited trepidation, I carefully packed it away in my school bag and walked home. Surely if Mum saw what an effort I'd gone to, she'd appreciate it.

Mum was in her bedroom when I let myself in the flat with my key and I didn't dare disturb her. I'd accidentally made that mistake before and she'd gone beserk. I waited patiently for her to come out a couple of hours later and shyly presented her with my card.

'I made this for you, Mummy.' I smiled at her from underneath my fringe, holding out the card.

She snatched it out of my hands, her lips twisting into a disgusted smirk. 'What is it supposed to be?'

I pointed to the picture. 'Look there's you and me and some flowers and–'

'It's rubbish!' she cut me off. 'Can't you do better

than that? Why are you so useless at everything?'

I stifled back the tears. I'd gone to so much trouble and felt sure she would be as happy with it as I was.

'Well, you've got another thing coming if you think I'm going to put that up in here.' She screwed the card into a ball and threw it in the bin, then rubbed her hands together as if the card was contaminated somehow and she was cleaning them. She turned to me with a vicious grin. 'Now, go and tidy the lounge up, it's a mess! If you leave your toys hanging around one more time, they'll go in the bin as well.

Shortly after that, we moved to another flat. I didn't know it at the time, but Mum didn't give Nan or Linda our address so she wouldn't come around asking any more questions. The new flat didn't have a telephone either, and I suspect this was so Nan wouldn't even be able to call and ask about my welfare.

I also started a new school and was nervous about what to expect. I was so worried about my appearance and the fact I hardly ever had any clean clothes that I started washing them at night in the kitchen sink with bars of soap or washing up liquid when Mum was passed out in her bedroom or on the sofa from drinking too much Brandy again. I'd hide the clothes at the back of the airing cupboard until they dried. Even though they were rumpled and not ironed, at least they smelt OK. I wanted to try and make myself look like a nice, clean girl who wasn't ugly or fat like she said so I tried my hardest to do my hair and look clean and tidy. If I could try and make myself look pretty, maybe she would be able to love me and not get so angry with me all the time. I longed for her to just give me praise, affection, and a kind word.

I preferred the new flat. It was only ten minutes walk to my school, and one of our neighbours had a tabby cat called Tigger that used to follow me in the mornings. I'd shoo her away as I was walking but she kept following me. It was only when we got to the school gates that she'd turn around and pad back towards the flats. When I came back from school, she was always waiting for me on the steps outside the flat and I'd play with her for a while, snuggling into her warm fur and wishing she was mine.

Jim knew how much I loved cats and one weekend he came home with a little kitten for me.

'Sarah,' he called out as he came through the front door. 'I've got a present for you, come and look.'

I ran into the hallway and saw him carrying a brown cardboard box.

'For me?' I asked shyly.

He nodded, grinning, and handed me the box.

I could hear a scratching sound and small meows coming from inside.

I glanced back up at him, seeking permission to open it and making sure it really was for me.

He nodded. 'Well, go on then. Open it.'

I undid the top of the box, holding my breath, almost not wanting the present to be a kitten in case I was mistaken or it was some cruel joke that Mum often liked to play on me. But no, inside was a tiny kitten, blinking at me with huge blue eyes and wriggling as she tried to reach up to me. I scooped up the warm bundle of fur in my arms and stroked her head.

I was ecstatic. A cat of my very own! I called her Dusty, in memory of the second soft toy Nan had bought me when she visited but had miraculously disappeared shortly afterwards. The kitten was mostly black with white socks on her feet and on the end of her tail, and she would follow me around the flat for hours. I was worried what Mum would do to her. After all, if she could do those things to her own daughter, what would she do to a poor, defenceless little kitten? But, surprisingly, Mum seemed to really like her. It was strange and deeply upsetting to see her showing so much affection to Dusty, often cuddling and kissing her, when she couldn't show even an ounce to her own daughter. Mum would always make sure she always had plenty of tins of cat food in the house, which was good for me because Mum still wasn't feeding me breakfast or dinner so I could eat spoonfuls of cat food when she wasn't looking. She made me keep Dusty's litter tray in my bedroom as she said, 'It always stinks of piss in there, anyway.' I didn't mind one bit, because it meant Dusty spent more time with me. At night she would snuggle up on my bed in the crook of my arm, licking me with her rough tongue and padding me with her paws. Instead of crying myself to sleep now, Dusty's purrs and cuddles send me off, comforting me in the lonely darkness.

# CHAPTER 5

The new flat marked the start of a relatively calm period in my life. One weekend when Jim was home, I heard the usual noises from their bedroom. After they'd finished moaning and groaning, Mum started crying loudly. It was especially memorable because I don't think I'd ever heard her cry before. I listened outside the room with Dusty winding her way in between my feet, insisting I feed her.

'I'm starting to hear things, Jim,' I heard her say.

'What sort of things, love?' he said.

She sniffed. 'Voices.'

'Don't worry, honey. Maybe it's a side effect of the anti depressants. We'll get you to the doctors and get you on some new medication. It will be OK, don't worry yourself about it,' he said.

I didn't know what the voices were that Mum was referring to, but that morning they left me in the flat to go to the doctors. When they came back Mum seemed happier. She stopped drinking brandy, started doing the washing again and cleaning the flat on a regular basis, and while she often forgot to feed me and still ignored me most of the time, at least she wasn't as violent. At that time, I would just get a smack on the bottom or around the face if I did something that annoyed her, like not cleaning the bathroom properly or forgetting to clean out Dusty's litter tray, but that was much better than all the other punishments she'd dished out before.

I started to enjoy school, too, and made a friend called Jenny who lived in the flats opposite ours. Mum even let me go and play with her after school and at the weekends. I think she liked the fact that I wasn't in the house all the time and it gave her more time to herself so she could get her nails and hair done and go shopping for new clothes.

For the first time since I'd lived with Nan, I got to see what a normal family was like. Jenny's mum made home-cooked dinners like spaghetti bolognese and cheese and onion pie, and there was always plenty to go around.

'You need fattening up a bit,' Jenny's mum said to me, always dishing up second helpings. 'Doesn't your mum feed you?'

Despite things being pretty good with Mum lately, I was still too scared to say anything to anyone in case she found out and the evil Mum returned.

Jenny had an older brother called Steve who hung out with his mates from the flats, tearing about the neighbourhood on the bicycles. Jenny had a bicycle, too, but she knew I didn't have one so she never rode it when I was with her. I wished Mum or Jim would buy me one so I could ride around, feeling the wind in my hair.

Jenny and I would play dress-up in her mother's old clothes, and I pretended to be a beautiful princess like Nan had always said. We'd play-act Cinderella and Sleeping Beauty, and for a moment I could forget about my life and feel safe cocooned in Jenny's family. At night I would dream that Jenny was really my sister but I'd been switched at birth and one day Jenny's mum would realise there had been a mistake and would bring me to live with her.

I stopped wetting the bed at that point and it was nice to go to school not smelling of wee or looking so different from the other kids because Mum began washing my clothes again. Instead of dwelling on what had happened in the past, I embraced my new life and started to feel happy again. I concentrated on reading and schoolwork, and the teachers praised me for being such a good student.

Mum got a new part time job as a waitress in a café near the flats, which meant that she'd often bring leftovers home for us to eat so I slowly started putting on weight again. She worked until eight o'clock at night, which meant I had plenty of freedom to play with Jenny and do my chores in peace.

Jim bought Mum a washing machine. It had lots of fancy dials and buttons on it, and she taught me how to use it. It would be my job to make sure the clothes were washed and hanging up on the radiators or airers around the flat. When they were dry I had to fold them neatly in a pile for her to iron, and she seemed to take pride again in me having clean clothes and keeping the flat tidy.

At the weekends, when Jim was home, he would take us for family outings to Buckingham Palace or the London Zoo. I loved all the animals and decided that one day I was going to be a vet.

This relatively idyllic time carried on for about

two years. Mum was having regular check ups at the hospital and she seemed to be much happier. I started to forget what Nan looked like, although I never stopped thinking about her and wondering if she thought about me. I was disappointed that she never came to see me again and that Mum wouldn't let me go and stay with her for holidays, but I didn't want to get Mum angry by talking about Nan.

One day Mum announced that she was pregnant and I would have a baby brother or sister. I was over the moon. I loved Jenny and Dusty, but I longed to have someone else to play with. My happiness was short lived, though. It wasn't long before the evil Mum returned. The nice Mum retreated into oblivion, only to be glimpsed occasionally for show.

# CHAPTER 6

Mum stopped taking her 'happy pills' when she was pregnant and pretty soon she was back to her old ways. I tried to creep around the house silently like a mouse, hoping to make myself invisible so she wouldn't notice me around. There was no one around to help me so I had to try and help myself by staying out of way as much as possible. It seemed like my mere presence would annoy her. The weight of her simmering anger was like a dark cloud, crushing me, lingering like a permanent shadow long after her initial outburst had finished. I would feel her hawk-eyes following me around, ever watchful, waiting for me to do something she didn't like.

She had a range of 'punishments' she would give me when she was angry with me. I had a permanent knot in my stomach all the time, and coupled with the hunger pains, at times I thought my stomach was being twisted in two.

If I didn't wash up the dishes properly after she made her dinner, she would hit me with a belt or slipper. If I didn't make a cup of tea to her liking, she would throw the hot liquid all over me. If I didn't do my chores properly, dusting or vacuuming the house, she would strangle me until I passed out. The first time this happened, I was so shocked and scared I couldn't even scream out.

I was dusting her wooden bookshelf that housed some china ornaments that my dad had given her, and was so worried about finishing them quickly so I could do my homework and not get into trouble at school that I missed one of the shelves.

After I moved onto polishing the TV, she stormed into the room to check what I was doing. Slowly she ran a fingertip along the bookshelf and examined her finger for dust.

'Why can't you do anything right, brat?' she hissed at me. 'My life was perfect before I had you and now look at things! Why are you doing this to me?'

But I didn't know what I was doing to her. All I ever did was what she ordered me to do.

My back stiffened, readying myself for what was to come, and Dusty, who was curled up on the sofa, shot out of the room. She'd become almost as good at anticipating Mum's moods as me. Mum pushed me hard, the ground coming up to meet me. The next minute she was on top of me, her knee pressing down on my chest with all her weight so I could hardly breathe and her hands around my throat.

I tried to fling my arms and legs around to get her off, panicking, but the more I fought, the more she seemed to enjoy it. Guttural sounds came from my throat as I gasped for air, gripped by a worse feeling of panic than I'd ever felt before. I grabbed at her fingernails digging into my skin but I was no match for her strength.

I stared into her eyes, which had a glazed expression, thinking *I'm going to die. This time she's really going to kill me like she promised.*

I heard ringing in my ears, like a distant school bell.

*Maybe I'd be better off dead. Anything is better than this.*

I stopped struggling, willing death to come and take me.

Then I slipped into unconsciousness.

I awoke to her slapping me around the face with a shocked expression. 'Wake up! Wake up, brat!'

My throat felt raw and dry as I inhaled deep gulps of air.

She sat back, panting almost as much as me. 'You stupid idiot! Look what you made me do now. Get out of my sight.'

I made my way to the bathroom on unsteady legs, holding onto the walls to support. Once inside, I stuck my head under the cold tap, swallowing as much water as I could, still trying to get my breath back at the same time, which made me choke even more.

After she realised that she could choke me to unconsciousness and I wouldn't die, she did it on a regular basis. In the past, if any of the teachers questioned the scratches and bruises on my body, I would have to tell them that I was really clumsy and kept falling off my bike or down the stairs, or I walked into doors accidentally, but Mum knew I wouldn't be able to explain the bruises on my neck as easily, so whenever she strangled me she kept me off school until the bruises faded.

Another favourite punishment of hers was making me swallow washing up liquid. I'd developed an obsession with cleanliness then, and had a habit of washing my hands all the time, often using up the last of washing up liquid or soap. Mum had given up work by then and was quite far along in her pregnancy so she was at home most of the time and I didn't seem to get much reprieve from her.

I was washing my hands at the kitchen sink after I'd put some washing in the machine and she stormed in, her face flushed, her lips contorted in an evil grin.

'Seeing as you like being clean so much, let's make sure your insides are clean, too.' She reached under the kitchen sink and pulled out a bottle of washing up liquid. 'Drink it,' she ordered.

I shook my head and screamed, 'NO!'

She slapped me around the face so hard my head swung back and hit the wall.

'Drink it!' she yelled. 'If you don't drink it, I'll just think of something else.'

'Please don't make me, mummy,' I whimpered.

She yanked on my hair, tipping my neck back, holding onto me so I couldn't get away. With the other hand, she poured the liquid into my mouth. I tried to clamp my lips together but she wasn't having any of it. She let go of my hair and prised my mouth open, forcing in the tip of the bottle. 'Swallow it!'

I started gagging and threw most of it back up. Then she stood back and surveyed the slippery mess of vomit and washing liquid on the floor and told me to clean it up.

As soon as she left the room I rinsed my mouth out and cleaned my teeth what seemed like a hundred times but I still couldn't get the taste out.

It didn't stop at washing up liquid, though. She would make me swallow cooking oil, Ajax cleaning liquid, rancid milk. She didn't go as far as making drink bleach after that day in the bath in case she had to take me to see the doctor again.

She no longer hid her violent outbursts when Jim was around, either. Although he'd never been particularly attentive to me in the past, he was still usually kind, but he was never on my side. As Mum's pregnancy progressed, he would have frequent talks with me when he came home at weekends, telling me not to be so naughty and to stop upsetting her.

'But why is she always so cross with me?' I asked. If I knew why, I could try harder to make her love me.

He shrugged his shoulders. 'You know she's got a bit of a temper. You need to try harder to please her,' he said.

Mum would be on at him constantly as soon as he walked in the door about how I'd done this wrong and that wrong and how she couldn't take it anymore. I don't know whether he really believed all the things Mum told him or if he just went along with her for a quiet life. Either way, I didn't have anyone to turn to or protect me. If Mum became violent with me when he was around, he'd just walk out of the room and let her get on with it. If he thought it was normal, too, then maybe it really was, although deep down I knew this wasn't a normal mother-daughter relationship. Spending time with Jenny who had a loving mum and dad made me realise this was very abnormal, and sometimes I would get angry with Jenny for having something that I didn't. I felt worthless, useless, ugly, fat, unloveable. If someone tells you these things often enough you start to believe it. And now Jim was letting her get away with everything in plain sight without challenging her or stopping her, I really believed that no one would ever help me.

# CHAPTER 7

I hoped things would different when the baby was born but they weren't. Because Mum smoked during the pregnancy, Kaley was pretty small and Mum was extra loving and protective towards her. I loved my sister as soon as they brought her home from the hospital, but I also felt jealousy towards her. Mum would constantly taunt me by saying things like, 'Isn't she a beautiful little princess? Not like you,' or 'Why did I have you when I've got Kaley?' or 'I love Kaley so much.' I tried to drown it out but it was hard to accept that Mum was capable of loving one daughter and not the other.

Jim would help Mum with the baby when he was home at weekends, but during the week, I would have to get up and feed her before school because Mum said she was tired. I'd creep into their bedroom and lift Kaley out of her cot, taking her to the lounge and setting her down in a carrycot in front of the TV so I could give her a bottle. Kaley sucked greedily on the teet with a happy twinkle in her eye and I'd feel instantly bad about being jealous of a helpless little baby.

One morning Kaley was sucking away as normal but nothing seemed to be coming out. I shook the bottle a few times but Kaley cried out an ear-piercing scream, which must've woken Mum up. She stormed into the room and pushed me over, knocking me into the corner of the coffee table head first. My eyebrow sliced open and blood poured down my face. Instinctively, I pressed my hand to my eye but the beige carpet was rapidly turning red as blood dripped onto it.

'Can't you do anything right?' she yelled at me, picking up Kaley and making soft cooing noises to her.

I rushed from the room, soaked some paper tissue in water, and leant over the kitchen sink, trying to clean up my eyebrow. A black lump was forming on it already and the blood didn't seem to stop. Surprisingly, even with the fresh wound, she let me go to school that day, yelling that she couldn't stand looking at me.

As I hurriedly got dressed for school, I tried to think up yet more excuses that I could give the teachers to explain the state of my eye. I knocked for Jenny so we could walk to school together, as usual, but her Mum opened the door instead, wiping her hands on a dishcloth. She gasped when she saw the state of me.

'Sarah, what happened?' She furrowed her eyebrows together, studying me so carefully I wondered if she could read my mind.

I glanced away quickly. 'Nothing,' I mumbled. 'I tripped over Kaley and fell into the edge of the coffee table.'

Her eyes searched mine for answers that I couldn't possibly give, then she tilted my head back to get a better look at my eye. Blood was still oozing down the side of my face and I had to keep wiping it away.

She frowned with concern. 'It looks like this needs stitches. Where's your mum?'

*Oh, God, no! She can't make a fuss about it with Mum. Please don't let her tell Mum!*

My heart beat so hard with worry that it felt like my chest was going to explode. 'Mum's busy with Kaley,' I said meekly. 'And it's not as bad as it looks.' I wiped my eye and stared at the blood on my fingers.

Jenny came to the door, her eyelids flying open and her jaw dropping at the state of my face. 'Are you all right? It looks really bad,' she said to me.

Something angry flashed in Jenny's mum's eyes for a minute before she said, 'Come inside,' She led me into the kitchen where she pulled out a first aid kit from one of the cupboards. Gently, she dabbed a dampened wad of cotton wool on the cut to clean it up a bit and cut a big piece of plaster off a roll to stick over my eyebrow. Because the blood was oozing so much, the plaster wouldn't stick so she found a clean tea towel, folded it up, and made me press it over the wound.

'Jenny, you head on off to school and I'll take Sarah to Casualty to get it stitched up,' her mum said.

'Can't I come with you,' Jenny asked.

'No. Go on now and do as you're told.'

'It's OK,' I insisted, not wanting to cause such a fuss. If Mum got to hear about it, she'd be livid. 'I'm sure it will stop bleeding soon.'

Jenny's mum slid her hand in mine and we caught the bus to the hospital.

As we sat in the Casualty department waiting to be seen by a doctor, I fidgeted nervously in my seat. It was the first time I'd ever been in a hospital and I was worried about what kind of questions they might ask me. Part of me wanted them to guess that my mum had done this to me so they could take me away from her, but part of me was so scared she'd find out I'd been telling tales and I got another round of strangling or beating. Plus, I was embarrassed about everything. Mum constantly drummed into me what a bad girl I was. How I was dirty, smelly, ugly, useless, fat, and could never do anything right. This was really all my fault. Even though she was so cruel, I loved her and had a strong desire to please her. She was the only mum I had, and I wanted to be a good girl so she'd love me like she did Kaley and Jim. When I look back now it seems so bizarre that I would want a mother like that to love me, but she was all I had. I was nine years old and didn't know what would happen to me if she threw me out onto the streets.

Jenny's mum started asking me all sorts of things about what was going on at home but, as usual, I had to lie to her. She didn't look very convinced by my answers. A young male doctor eventually called my name and I was relieved that it meant I wouldn't have to answer her probing questions anymore.

As he examined me, I got more questions from him about how it had happened. Jenny's Mum and doctor exchanged suspicious glances at my answers but didn't say anything. After he'd stitched me up, he told me to go and sit in the waiting room while he talked to Jenny's mum.

*Oh, no. I've really done it now. Mum will find out and kill me for sure.*

But when Jenny's mum reappeared she didn't say anything about what they'd discussed. She bought me some sweets on the way home and dropped me off at school.

All through the day I constantly worried that Jenny's Mum or the doctor would say something to Mum and I'd be in serious trouble. I watched the clock turning around all day, and when the bell finally rang, I walked back home with Jenny chattering away as usual without a care in the world, oblivious to my state of inner turmoil.

'What's the matter?' Jenny finally asked me because I kept answering her back in monosyllables.

'Oh, nothing. I've just got a bit of a headache, that's all,' I lied.

I stood on the concrete steps at the entrance to the flats, my legs trembling, before taking a deep breath and going inside.

Mum must've been waiting for me, and hearing my key turn in the lock, she stormed down the hallway, grabbed me by the throat and threw me up against the wall.

'Why have you been telling lies about me, you stupid bitch? I've had that nosy kid's mum round here asking me all sorts of questions about you!' She squeezed my throat as hard as she could so it was impossible to breathe. 'You ungrateful cow! Is this how you repay me for giving birth to you?'

I clutched at her hands, trying to prise them off but the grip was too strong. I felt myself slipping into unconsciousness when she suddenly let go, panting and swearing at me. 'What did you tell her?'

I crouched down on the floor and clutched my raw throat, too scared to move.

She picked me up by the shoulders and shook me so hard I could feel my brain rattling around.

'Answer me!' she screamed. 'What did you tell her?'

But I couldn't answer. I could hardly breathe let alone speak.

'I've warned you before not to tell anyone. Do you think they'll believe what you say?' She let go of me and scowled, her tone mocking. 'Do you really think they'll listen to a useless, fat brat? It's all your fault. Everything's your fault!'

I willed the tears not to fall. I wouldn't give her the satisfaction.

'Think you can go behind my back, do you?' she carried on.

'I didn't say anything, mummy, honestly,' I managed to croak out.

Then she stood back with a scary smile on her face and said, 'No one's going to come and rescue you, you pathetic little brat. Now go to your room.' She pointed down the hallway and I stumbled into my bedroom. She slammed the door shut and I heard the lock turn in the key, sealing me in my prison.

As soon as the door closed the tears fell so I didn't notice Dusty at first because my vision was blurred.

As I sat down next to her on the bed, she didn't move. Usually, she would jump into my lap and start purring so I knew something was wrong. Her eyes were open, staring blankly into space, and her neck was at an odd angle. I tried to pick her up for a cuddle but she was stiff and heavy and she wasn't breathing.

I let out an anguished cry as I curled up in a ball around Dusty's lifeless body.

'Aw…is the brat upset?' Mum called in a sarcastic tone through my bedroom door. 'Are you going to be a cry-baby all night?'

For the first time in my life I felt pure anger and hatred towards my mum, and for years afterwards I had recurring nightmares about finding Dusty like that. I sobbed into my pillow that night so she couldn't hear me. To anyone else, Dusty would've been just a cat, but to me, she was one of my best friends. The only one who tried to comfort me when I was at my lowest. The only other witness to my horrible life. It seemed that everything and everyone I loved was taken away from me. Not only had Mum succeeded in killing my beloved cat, she was also killing my spirit.

# CHAPTER 8

The following morning Mum unlocked my bedroom door and told me I wasn't going to school anymore and I had to start helping her pack. We were moving again. I wanted to bury Dusty outdoors somewhere nice, like in the local park, but I didn't have a shovel and I didn't want to speak to Mum to ask her if I could. I knew she'd refuse anyway.

Half way through the day, after I'd piled sheets and clothes into boxes and suitcases, I went into the kitchen to get a drink of water, since that was all Mum would let me have, and I noticed she'd put Dusty in the bin. My precious friend was thrown away like a useless piece of rubbish. From that moment on, I vowed never to let her know when I cared about something because she would take it away from me. Dusty had been cruelly taken away from me, and since we were moving again, I'd also be losing my best friend, Jenny. I never got to even say goodbye to Jenny and her family.

Jim used his work lorry to move our furniture and belongings from London to a village in Bedfordshire. We drove through small countr y lanes that were only just about wide enough for the lorry, and a couple of times I thought we'd actually get stuck. We finally arrived at a small council house right on the edge of the village about half a mile from any other houses. On the one hand, I was excited about living in a house with a garden in the country instead of in a flat, but on the other hand, I was worried that because it was secluded, no one would be able to hear me screaming. Not that that had made much difference before. When we lived in the different flats none of the neighbours intervened when they heard my screams and beatings. No one seemed to want to get involved with what went on behind closed doors, apart from Jenny's Mum, of course. Mum and Jim made a concerted effort to keep people at arm's length, hardly ever venturing out into the village except for essential shopping. They never seemed to have any friends or feel the need for any.

As I stared at my new home, I wondered if us moving there would make things any better. Would a fresh start make Mum love me?

The house was browny-grey with small pebbles on the outer walls and a big overgrown garden that backed onto some woods. Inside the paint was flaking off the ceiling and windows and the wallpaper hung off the walls. There was damp in some of the rooms and it had a musty, unlived in smell. The garden was overgrown with weeds and the whole place had an eerie feel to it. I heard Mum and Jim saying that no one else wanted to live there because it was so run down, but Jim said he'd be able to do it up at the weekends when he was off work.

True to his word, Jim would arrive home on his days off to tackle a new DIY job. After I'd done my homework, one of my chores was to help him on whatever project he was doing. I spent hours stripping wallpaper, sanding down the wooden window frames and floorboards, and painting the walls. When the house was eventually finished, it was transformed into a bright, cosy house with tranquil views – the complete opposite of my life. My small bedroom overlooked the woods and I often fantasised about running away and hiding myself in them forever.

I started a new school in the village and would walk the lonely mile every morning in the rain and snow. Mum was being more careful now not to cause any bruises to my face and neck because she didn't want anyone at the new school asking more questions about us.

On the way to school one morning, I saw that one of the fields was full of sheep with their little baby lambs. As I approached them, I noticed one of the lambs had got its head stuck inside a gap in the chicken wire fence and it was bleating away, trying to tug free. Its mum stood next to it, bleating back and fussing around it, nuzzling and pushing it as if trying to help her baby get free. I knelt down and managed to stretch the wire, pushing the lamb's small head out gently. The sheep licked her lamb a few times before nudging it back to the safety of the field. My eyes watered with unshed tears. Even that sheep was a better mum than mine was.

Instinctively, knew I didn't fit in at my new school. The other kids arrived every morning in crisp, clean uniforms with their shiny hair in smooth ponytails and bunches tied with ribbons, their cheeks full of colour. I arrived, pale and unkempt, wearing ill-fitting clothes with tangled hair. Whenever I tried to do my hair like theirs, it always ended up looking a mess. They could sense that I was different to them, even at that age. Maybe they could smell my fear and feel the vulnerability and weakness permeating from me like vultures sensing when something has died, swooping in to satisfy their hunger. When they weren't calling me names or taunting me, they would give me a wide birth and ignore me. At break times I'd take a book and sneak out to the furthest corner of the playground and sit down, trying to drown out the sound of their laughter and ignore the happy smiles on their faces. Eventually, I did make friends with a girl called Becky, but whenever she would ask me to go and play at her house I would always have to refuse. I was hardly ever allowed out of the house apart from school, and at weekends I would have to help Jim with the redecorating. But even though the kids didn't like me, I loved school. It was the only place I go to escape home for six hours a day, and I immersed myself in books. Every time I chose a new book from the school library, I found an exciting world that I could daydream about. I loved Gulliver's Travels and Enid Blyton's Famous Five series, which seemed to give me hope that one day I'd escape from Mum and have a new, happy life. It was a dream I desperately clung on to, and when I was getting a beating, I would go to a special place in my mind, running far away from Mum into one of the adventures I'd read about so that the reality of my life wouldn't cause me so much pain.

Some of the kids brought packed lunches to school instead of having school dinners, and every morning before they sat down they would have to put their lunch boxes on a table in the corner of the room. Mum still didn't let me have any breakfast, and often I would have to make do with only the scraps from her dinner in the evenings so most of the time I was starving. After morning break, I would try and sneak into the classroom early so I could steal something from the lunch boxes and scoff it down before anyone else came in. Often I managed a biscuit or an apple to stave off the hunger pains until it was time to have my school lunch, burying the wrappers in the bottom of the teacher's bin so she wouldn't notice. Slowly, the other kids in the class began to realise things were going missing and must've complained to the teacher. One day, I snuck into the classroom early and helped myself to a bar of chocolate, shoving it in my mouth and swallowing it so quickly it hardly had time to touch the sides. I was burying the wrapper in the bin, as usual, when I glanced out of the classroom window and saw my teacher staring at me, arms folded, a pinched expression on her face.

*Oh, no. I'm really in for it now.*

I wished the ground would open up and swallow me.

I sat down at my desk, shaking and waiting for her to come and shout at me. I knew she'd tell Mum and then I'd be in even worse trouble. It seemed to take an eternity for her to make her way into the classroom, and as she stepped inside the room and shut the door, I could hear the other kids piling up behind it with boisterous chatter.

Slowly, she sat down at my desk, giving me a cold stare. 'You're the one who's been stealing from the lunch boxes all along, aren't you?'

I nodded. 'I'm sorry.'

'Why?' she barked at me.

*Because I'm starving. Because my mum hates me and can't be bothered to feed me. Because the pains in my stomach keep me awake at night.*

Couldn't she see that I was literally skin and bones?

'I'm really sorry,' I said again, looking down at my shoes and avoiding her angry stare.

She stood up and said with contempt, 'What makes you think it's right to steal from other people's lunches?'

'It's not right. I'll never do it again,' I said.

'Why didn't you own up when I made an announcement to the class last week?'

I couldn't answer her.

'Stealing is a serious crime and I need to think of a suitable punishment,' she said, pausing for a moment. 'Since you didn't own up when you had the chance, every break time for a week you'll be inside writing out lines about why it's wrong to steal.' She let that sink in for a moment and then said, 'And think yourself lucky we won't be calling the police.'

I exhaled a breath of relief. Lines were easy.

'I'll be sending a letter home to your mother to let

69

her know about your despicable behaviour as well,' she carried on.

'Please, miss. Please don't tell her.'

She narrowed her eyes at me. 'We have a duty to let your mother know what's been going on.'

*What about a duty to me? What about a duty to protect me?*

She wagged her finger at me, a red flush creeping up her neck with rage. 'And don't let me catch you doing it again.'

Becky didn't want anything to do with me after that. All the other kids already thought I was weird because I was dressed in untidy clothes and didn't play with them after school or get invited to birthday parties. Now they thought I was a liar and a thief, too, and they all started making fun of me. Although their names couldn't hurt me like Mum's abuse, I was devastated because even though school wasn't great, it was my sanctuary – a place where I could have at least some respite from being treated like dirt. Now, I was subjected to taunts and bullying at school as well as at home. I wanted to die, and dreaded every school day looming ahead.

I was also petrified about what would happen when the teacher told Mum what I'd done. All that week, I crept in from school, worrying that they'd written to her, but I seemed to have been granted a miracle because nothing happened.

Then, as Saturday morning rolled around, a letter arrived addressed to Mum from the school.

I was helping Jim paint the garden fence outside when I heard her yelling for me to come in the house.

My stomach sank to the bottom of my feet, wondering what she was going to do now.

I glanced at Jim nervously, tremors shaking my whole body.

'You're always causing trouble,' he said. 'Why do you always have to upset your mum? Haven't you made her suffer enough? You know she has to take her medication because of you,' he said impatiently.

And that's when I finally got it. She blamed me for everything. It was my fault I'd made her depressed when I was born, and it was my fault my dad had left her alone because he was travelling to visit me at Nan's house when he was hit by a car and died. Her life would've still been perfect if I hadn't been around. How many times had she told me that? Over the years her bitterness and resentment towards me had magnified a hundred times over.

'Well, go on! See what she wants.' He jerked his head in the direction of the house.

I went into the house and found Mum pacing up and down the lounge, waving the letter around.

When she saw me, she grabbed my jaw in her fingers and started squeezing. 'What have you been up to now? You got caught stealing! Stealing! You little thief!' She kept repeating the word 'thief' over and over again as if stealing a chocolate bar was a really terrible crime but beating her child wasn't. 'Well, if you're so hungry you need to steal a chocolate bar, come and have something to eat.' She pulled me along by my jaw into the kitchen and threw the lid off the bin. It hit the floor with an echoing clang.

She pushed my face inside the bin, which smelt rancid and decaying. There were potato peelings, apple cores, bits of tissue paper that had Kaley's snot on them, tea bags, gristle from the steak she'd cooked herself the night before.

'Go on, then,' she said in a mocking voice. 'If you're so hungry, eat it.'

I hesitated, knowing she wouldn't let me go until I'd done as she'd said, and if I didn't eat it, I'd just get more punishment.

'If you don't eat it now, you'll have to eat it tomorrow when it's even more rotten,' she teased.

As I chewed on the dirty peelings and tissue under her unwavering stare, I tried to imagine that this was some delicious delicacy from one of the exotic destinations I'd read about in my books.

One good thing did come out of it, though. After that, she started letting me have an apple or bowl of porridge for breakfast in case somebody started asking questions.

# CHAPTER 9

Things got worse still, though, when she started including Jim in my punishments. By using Kaley as a weapon, Mum made him complicit in our abusive world. It started off by him putting a hand over my mouth if I screamed when she punched or kicked me. Later, it progressed to him spanking me with his belt. Usually, I heard the snapping of his belt before he shouted for me to come into the kitchen. I would freeze, wondering what lies Mum had made up about me now. Sometimes I wouldn't be able to sit down properly for a week.

I was watching TV one morning when I heard raised voices in the kitchen as Mum told Jim that I'd put a cushion over Kaley's face. I sat as still as a rock, waiting for what I knew would come.'

'SARAH!' Jim called from the kitchen. 'Get in here now!'

Obediently, I went in. Jim was fuming, his face pink with anger and his eyes bulging. Mum stood leaning against the fridge, her lips twisted in that satisfied smile.

'I will not tolerate you taking out your jealousy on Kaley,' Jim said to me. 'Who do you think you are, hurting my poor defenceless baby?'

I cowered in the doorway. 'But I didn't do anything,' I whispered. 'I love Kaley. Why would I put a cushion over her face?'

'Don't answer him back,' Mum snapped.

'Your mum told me what you did.' He snapped the belt he had in his hand.

'She needs punishing, Jim,' Mum egged him on.

'Bend over the table,' he said to me.

I bent over the edge of the kitchen table and he pulled my skirt up and my knickers down. I put my hands over my exposed bottom to try and protect myself but Mum roughly pulled my hands away.

*Why is she lying? Why is this happening to me? Why don't they love me? Why doesn't anyone notice and do something? What can I do to stop all the pain?*

As I turned my head to the side, shaking with embarrassment, shame, and fear, I caught site of Mum smiling at him and nodding her encouragement.

I felt the first crack on my bottom and a lightening bolt of hot flames on my skin. I screamed out in pain, but Mum forced her hand over my mouth to shut me up with one hand and held me down with the other.

More forceful blows reigned down on me, my whole body shaking as the sounds of my screams filtered through her fingers. By bottom was on fire and I could feel the wet sticky blood oozing down the back of my legs. I wiggled and struggled for all I was worth but I was no match for two adults.

It was only Kaley's cries that saved me from more. As soon as she made a sound from their bedroom, they both rushed out of the room to check she was OK and left me collapsed over the table.

Dazed, I sloped off to the bathroom to cleanse my wounded skin with soap and warm water, trying to make sense of it all and recover emotionally and physically from all that had happened that day.

# CHAPTER 10

My birthday came and went again with no celebrations and not even a card. I was eleven years old, and little more than a slave and a punching bag. Every morning before school, I would have to do housework and feed Kaley because Mum hated getting up early. After school, I would have more chores and homework. At the weekends, I had to help Jim doing odd jobs around the house. Nothing I did ever seemed to be right for Mum, and she would come up with anything as an excuse to torture me mentally or physically.

Kaley was two and had reached the 'terrible twos' stage. If she couldn't have what she wanted she would throw a tantrum and start hitting me like she'd seen Mum and Jim do. Mum thought it was hilarious. Kaley was always spared physical abuse from Mum, and although I still felt jealous of her, she was my little sister and I loved her to bits. It didn't help that Mum encouraged Kaley to hit or kick me when she was in one of her moods. Jim had stopped buying me clothes and presents years ago, so I looked terrible in my second-hand clothes, but they always spent money on themselves and Kaley, making sure she had the best of everything.

The good thing about my birthday meant that after the school summer holidays, I would be starting secondary school and would hopefully make some new friends who didn't know about my past and wouldn't judge me by how I looked.

On the first day of my new school, I took a lot of care getting ready. I was now getting more aware of my developing body and I wanted to look nice, not like the 'weird' kid that I'd always been before. I had to make do with a uniform that was far too big for me because Mum said I would grow into it. I tied a belt around the skirt on its tightest notch to stop it falling down when I walked. I brushed my long hair in the mirror until it shone, trying to make myself look pretty, but all I could see staring back at me was an ugly, fat girl that no one would like.

Mum leant against the bathroom door, smirking at me as I brushed my hair. 'I don't know why you're bothering with your hair. It just looks like rat's tails. Trying to impress the boys, are you?'

*Please don't do anything to me this morning on my first day of school. Please just leave me alone for once.*

Eventually she got bored and went to play with Kaley, and I exhaled a breath of relief that I wasn't even aware I was holding.

I nervously got on the school bus, wondering if the other kids would be able to tell my horrible secrets just by looking at me. I sat down next to a girl already there who looked the same age as me with ginger curly hair, freckles, and sparkling eyes.

'Hi, I'm Amy.' She grinned at me.

'Sarah.' I grinned back.

'Are you just starting the first year?' she asked.

'Yes.' I nodded.

'Me too!'

Luckily, we were put in the same class, and Amy and I giggled our way through our first day. When I got home, Mum was waiting for me like a caged tiger, ready to pounce.

'Get in here now!' she screamed from the kitchen,

I felt paralysed.

'Where are you? When I tell you to do something, do it!'

I had an overwhelming urge to run back out the door but where would I go? I would just be prolonging the inevitable and making it a hundred times worse when I had to come back. It would be hopeless.

Like a puppet on an invisible string, I walked towards her anger, as usual, awaiting my fate with wobbling knees.

She grabbed me by the hair and dragged me across the kitchen so hard that it felt like lumps of hair were being pulled out. My body went rigid with pain and fear.

'Think you look nice, do you? You're nothing but a tart! That hair of yours needs cutting. It's a mess.' She pushed me down into a chair at the table and hacked at my hair with a pair of kitchen scissors.

I felt numb inside. I didn't think there was anything she could do to me that hadn't already been done, but because I was getting older and wanted to appear normal, at least from the outside, I wanted to fit in with the other school kids by looking like them. There was no mirror for me to see what it looked like, but I knew that Mum would try and make it as horrible as possible. Once again, she was doing her best to make me the 'weird' kid and alienate me from having friends.

I watched my lovely long waves drop onto the floor. A cool breeze from the open door blew on my now naked neck and my head instantly felt lighter.

When she finished, she walked around me with a smirk on her face, surveying her handiwork. Then she nodded slowly, very satisfied with herself. 'There, that's much better.' She pointed to the hair on the floor. 'Now clean it up and then you can do your chores.'

As she left the room, I swept up my long, lifeless hair, letting it slip through my fingers, dreading going to school the next day. I looked in the bathroom mirror and gasped in horror. I looked like a boy. My hair was chopped about with a wonky fringe and uneven sides.

I'd become quite good at compartmentalising my feelings. Over the years, when Mum was abusing me, I'd learnt to drift off to another place until it was over, but somehow, this was even worse than the beatings. I could hide the beatings inside. I could cover most of the scars and bruises, but everyone would notice my hair and see me looking like a freak. Yet again, I'd have no friends. What was left of my spirit seemed to disappear into thin air like my hair. That was the first time I contemplated suicide.

That night as I lay in bed, staring at the ceiling and worrying what taunts everyone at school would come up with, I thought about ways I could escape my life for good. Mum and Jim obviously didn't want me. I was useless, pathetic, ugly, and fat. I could never do anything right. Who would ever want someone like me? I was unlovable. I was worse than a piece of dog's muck that people scraped off their shoe. I was a nothing. If I killed myself, at least I'd finally get some peace. My whole life flashed through my mind like a film on a continuous loop: the beatings, starvation, Dusty, the taunts, the vicious punishments. I would be better off dead.

After Mum and Jim went to bed, I crept into the kitchen and found a bottle of Paracetamol that they kept at the back of the drawer. With silent tears streaming down my face, I swallowed them one by one, trying not to gag. I don't know how many I took, but I went back to bed, waiting for oblivion to overtake me. I lay down on my bed, feeling drowsy, thinking of Nan and Linda and Dusty, and how no one could save me.

# CHAPTER 11

I don't know how they found out what I'd done. Maybe Mum and Jim discovered the bottle of Paracetamol in the kitchen during the night. Maybe they had some kind of sixth sense. What I do know is that I woke up in hospital.

As my vision swam before my eyes, I could make out several doctors and nurses looming over me. I felt the prick of a needle in my arms and a doctor forcing a tube down my throat so they could flush out my stomach, then hands forcing me to sit up so I could be sick over and over again into a plastic bowl.

When I was spent, I finally noticed Mum looking on, glaring daggers at me when the nurses and doctors weren't looking and pretending to be fraught with worry.

'I don't know why she's done this,' Mum repeated over and over again to anyone who'd listen.

I wanted to scream at her what a liar she was in front of them all, but I felt too ill and too scared and exhausted. I wanted to slip into blank darkness where she couldn't hurt me anymore and I could just forget. I'd tried to kill myself and failed. I really was useless like she said because I couldn't even seem to do that right. Why didn't the medical staff notice the bruises and scars on my body and realise something was severely wrong? What would it take for people to open their eyes and notice?

After what seemed like hours of throwing up, I was wheeled into a private room on one of the wards and fell into a deep sleep. I awoke the next morning with a thumping headache and still feeling very nauseas. A doctor came in to examine me and ask questions as Mum sat in a chair next to my bed, giving him a faked look of worry.

He checked my notes and sat down on the bed. He had a mop of grey hair and thick, bushy eyebrows that he furrowed together as he studied me with a stern expression on his face.

He introduced himself as a psychiatrist and said, 'Now, then, young lady, what's been going on? Why did you take the tablets?'

I opened my mouth to speak but my throat was so sore and parched from the tube and vomiting that I had to keep swallowing to bring back some moisture.

Mum instantly leapt up from her chair and poured me a glass of water from the jug on the nightstand, just like an over-concerned Mum. She handed it to me with her back to the doctor so he couldn't see her face and mouthed, 'Tell no one.'

The weight of her stare and the seeds of rage simmering underneath it pinned me to the bed before she sat down again, smiling at me with a look of concern for him to see. After he waited for me to drink a few sips, he pressed me again.

'This is a very serious matter. I need to establish what happened,' he said. 'Why did you take the tablets?'

*Because I wanted to escape this hell! Because I don't think I can cope with this any longer. Because no one cares if I die.*

I wanted to tell him everything that had happened to me in my sad, pathetic life but what could I do? Mum was right beside me, acting like the perfect mother.

'It was an accident,' I croaked.

'An accident?' He raised one of his bushy eyebrows thoughtfully. 'So you didn't actually mean to kill yourself?'

I glanced briefly out of the corner of my eye. She was sitting there smiling at him. A smile I knew would slip off her face as soon as he left the room, only to be replaced again when there was a new audience.

'No,' I said.

'So, why did you take them?' he pressed me.

'I thought they were vitamin tablets,' I lied, like I'd been trained to do so well over the years.

'Hmm.' He sat back and studied me. 'And why would you take so many vitamin tablets?' there was a hint of sarcasm in his voice.

I shrugged, not knowing how to get myself out of the hole I'd just dug.

'What are you unhappy about?' he asked.

Where could I even start? 'I'm not unhappy,' I said, fiddling with the corner of my blanket and avoiding his nerve-wracking gaze. I blushed with shame.

'Can you think of a reason why she would intentionally take these tablets?' he asked Mum.

'Absolutely not, doctor,' she said. 'She's just started a new school so that could be it. You know how children can worry about fitting in at a new place.'

I stared at her, willing her to tell the truth for once.

He pointed to my hair. 'Did she do this to herself?' he asked her.

Mum reached out a ruffled my hair in a show of affection. 'Yes, the silly girl.'

'If we release you, will you try again?' he asked me.

'Try what again?' I asked, still wanting to make him believe it was an accident.

He sighed impatiently. 'Will you try to commit suicide again?'

I shook my head. 'It was an accident. It won't happen again.'

He stood up and said to Mum, 'Can I speak to you outside?'

She smoothed down her immaculate skirt and followed him into the corridor.

I couldn't hear what they said but after about ten minutes, he left and she came back in the room with her dagger-like glare locked in place. 'How could you do this to me? This is so embarrassing. Why can't you ever behave?' she hissed, her face inches away from mine so I could smell the stale cigarette smoke on her breath.

*Do this to her?! What about what you're doing to me?*

I glanced down at the blanket again, trying to avoid her eyes.

'You're allowed to go home now, but if you try anything like this again, they'll have you put into the loonie wing and you'll never get out. Maybe I should let them put you in there and get you off my hands. God knows I deserve a break from you.' She gave me a malicious grin. 'Or better still, why not try again and get it right next time.'

Mum kept me off school for a few days and pretty much ignored me. When the time came to go back to school, I was filled with a sense of dread about my appearance. I hung around down the road from the bus so I wouldn't have to wait with all the other kids. As I saw it round the corner, I ran towards it, jumping on just before the doors closed. I flopped down in the empty seat next to Amy and looked straight ahead, trying to ignore the sniggers from the kids behind. I heard shouts of 'Baldie,' and 'Kojak,' and 'Is that a girl or a boy?'

Amy gripped my arm, her mouth wide open. 'What happened to your hair?'

'My mum did it,' I said solemnly, feeling like I'd won one small victory by telling someone for once. 'Everyone's going to tease me now.'

I expected her to start laughing or calling me names, too, like the other kids were doing. I waited, my stomach churning with anxiety, until she picked up a clump of her long ginger curls and said, 'Hey, it could be worse, you could be a ginger mophead.'

We looked at each other and burst out laughing, and from that day on, she became my best friend, sitting next to each other in class and hanging out together at break and lunchtimes, but every time she asked me to go to her house for tea or a sleepover at the weekends, I'd have to make up excuses. I hated lying to her, and I desperately wanted to blurt out the truth about what happened at home, but Mum's threats of telling no one always screamed in my head. I was in her complete control, powerless to do anything to stop her.

# CHAPTER 12

It wasn't long after my suicide attempt that I developed anorexia. At the time, I didn't know there was a name for it. I felt empty inside. I was tired of having no real life to speak of. Tired of being beaten or ignored or ridiculed all the time. Tired of having no freedom. Just plain tired of it all. Yes, I had Amy at school and I was excelling in my work, but even that was a small sliver of light in the midst of so much darkness. I had no control over my life. Everything was dictated by how Mum felt at that particular time. Her moods controlled my happiness and my sorrow. The only thing I could control was what I ate. I think it was my small act of rebellion against her.

Over the years, I was used to not having enough food, so the hunger pains were pretty normal for me and I could easily ignore them. If I stopped eating, maybe I'd just wither away and die and everyone would be happy.

It was easy not to eat anything for breakfast. Mum never got up before I left for school so it's not like she noticed or would care anyway. At school, instead of having chips and baked beans and a burger, I'd grab something from the salad bar since

I knew that didn't have many calories. On the very rare occasions that Mum made dinner for me, I would push it around my plate and pick at it. Mostly, I was left to make a sandwich or toast for myself but I stopped using butter and just ate the bread dry.

I became obsessed with jumping on the scales to see how much weight I'd lost, and every morning before school, I'd sneak into the bathroom and stare at the dial, pleased that it kept going down and down. At least Mum wouldn't be able to call me fat anymore.

Although I never told Amy any details about what happened at home, she guessed that things weren't quite right. She noticed that I was losing weight and often brought in an extra bar of chocolate or packet of crisps for me to eat during break, but I would think up excuses not to eat them in front of her like, 'Mum cooked me a big breakfast this morning and I'm still really full,' or 'Thanks, I'll eat them a bit later on.' Then I'd throw them in the bin as I walked home from the school bus stop.

By the time my ribs and hip bones began sticking out and my cheeks became gaunt, Mum finally realised something wasn't quite right.

'What the hell's going on, with you?' she screamed at me one day when I was in the bath. 'What are you trying to do to me now? I'm sick and tired of you. Why can't you be a good girl like Kaley?'

I tried to cover up my skinny frame with my hands but she slapped them away, taking great delight in seeing me squirm with fear and embarrassment.

She pulled me out of the bath by my arm so hard I heard a cracking sound in my shoulder and dragged me into the kitchen naked. Forcing me into the chair that seemed to be my regular torture zone, she banged my head against the table so hard I saw stars and my tooth cut my lip.

'You think if you get thin enough they'll take you away, do you?' She laughed in my face, her eyes burning with hatred. 'Do me a favour! You must be crazy if you think people would actually want you.'

I started to think that maybe I was going crazy. Maybe she was the normal one and I was mad. A freak of nature that made her hate me.

She made me sit in the chair as she fried up three eggs, some bacon, and fried bread. She slopped it all on a plate and almost threw it in front of me. 'Eat that.'

I didn't even want to think about how many calories were in it, but I knew I'd have to eat it all. It was the most amount of food I'd seen on one plate for a long time and the thought of putting the greasy eggs and bacon in my mouth made me feel dirty inside. I hesitated as she lit up a cigarette.

She took a big puff and jabbed me with the end of the cigarette on my shoulder. The pain was incredible. I leapt up from the chair but she forced me back down.

She grinned sadistically at me. 'From now on, if I catch you not eating, you'll get burnt.'

Slowly, I picked up a knife and fork and cut the food into small pieces, but it obviously wasn't quick enough for her liking and she jabbed me again with the cigarette, this time on my back. She'd suddenly done an about turn, and instead of trying to starve me, at every available opportunity she would force me to eat. Slowly, I learnt to hide things better, and after her nightly ritual of forcing me to eat or burning me, I would find a way to sneak into the bathroom and be sick or I'd throw up in a plastic bag in my room and hide it in the bottom of the bin.

A few weeks later, she ordered me to make a sandwich for my dinner. She stood in the corner of the kitchen, arms folded, eyes narrowed, waiting for me to do something wrong. I could feel the tension in the air coming from her, like a contained bush fire that suddenly sparks out of control. I was always nervous and jittery around her, worried that anything I might do would set her off. There seemed to be no right or wrong as far as she was concerned and the slightest thing could make her angry with me. I tried to second-guess what she was thinking all the time so I could spare myself some of her fury. If I always did everything she wanted, exactly how she wanted, surely she would stop hurting me. But there seemed to be no pattern to it. Something as simple as breaking a nail or running out of milk would be my fault and could get her going on one of her furious frenzies.

I cut the loaf of bread slowly, the knife shaking in my hands, then wiped the breadboard of any crumbs. I was turning to get the butter from the fridge when she lurched forward and picked up the bread knife, holding it to my throat as she held me tightly from behind.

I gasped with shock, standing stock-still to

prevent the blade cutting into my skin.

'You've left crumbs on the breadboard,' she hissed in my ear, pressing the blade against my neck. 'Do you expect me to clean up after you? You're nothing but an ungrateful, dirty brat!'

I couldn't speak for fear the knife would dig in and cut me, but not answering her seemed to enrage her even more.

'What do you say?' she yelled.

'S…sorry,' I whispered.

'I could make you sorry right now.' She pressed the knife harder so I could feel a trickle of blood running down my neck. 'I could kill you easily and my life would be so much better without you. Shall I do it? All my problems would be over if I got rid of you.'

I whimpered in response, holding my breath, waiting for the moment when she sliced my neck in two. Maybe it would be better if she killed me and got it over with.

Finally, after what seemed like an eternity, she removed the knife from my skin and threw it in the sink with a loud clattering noise. 'Now, clear up this mess! Make one more mistake and I'll make you wish you'd never been born,' she barked and stormed out of the room.

But I already did wish I'd never been born.

# CHAPTER 13

Life carried on as it had always done and barely a day went by that I wasn't on the receiving end of one of Mum's punishments, but soon I had a new outlet. I developed a love of drama. It was the one lesson at school that I could lose myself in completely. When I acted out a part, I could pretend to be someone else instead of the geeky girl who burrowed herself in books so the other kids thought I was a teacher's pet. For a few hours in drama I could be a rich girl who had loving parents and flew off to exotic holidays in the summer holidays, or the most popular girl in the school who was trendy and always had lots of party invites. I could be anyone, as long as it wasn't me.

After I turned twelve, the drama teacher said he was going to put on an end of year show for the parents. We were going to act out Grease! I'd seen the film once on the TV and would pretend to be Sandy as I sung into a hairbrush in my bedroom. I would imagine I had a handsome guy like Danny who was in love with me and wanted to rescue me from Mum's clutches. When the teacher began auditions for Sandy, I was so excited. The song I chose to sing was *Look at me, I'm Sandra Dee* because the first few lines seemed like they were about me…

### *Look at me, there has to be*
### *Something more than what they see*

The drama teacher, My Hyde, settled onto his chair in front of the school stage with a clipboard resting on his knee and a pencil tucked behind his ear. The other kids in our class sat behind, watching the auditions and taking bets on who would make the lead roles.

'Sarah!' he called out my name. 'You're next.'

Amy gave me a big thumbs-up. 'Break a leg!'

I climbed the steps up to the stage with nervous anticipation and grabbed the microphone as all eyes rested on me.

The music teacher sat at a piano by the side of the stage and began the intro. I took a deep breath and belted out the song, completely immersing myself in the music and forgetting all my worries. For those few moments, I *was* Sandra Dee. When I finished, everyone clapped and cheered, and I felt like the most important little girl in the world.

We had to wait a week to find out which kids were going to play the various parts and it seemed to drag on forever. Finally, Mr Hyde called out our names one by one. I was going to play Sandy.

Amy hugged me and we gave each other high fives. Now all I had to do was convince Mum to let me do it because it was going to be an after school performance and I was hardly ever allowed out. The problem was, if she knew I really wanted something, she'd go out of her way to ruin it for me, so I didn't really hold out much hope of her agreeing.

That afternoon, I finished my chores and homework and struck up the courage to ask her about it. Surprisingly, she said yes immediately. It almost seemed to easy, like it was some kind of trap.

Over the next few months the whole class practiced songs and dance moves and for the first time in my life I felt like I really belonged. The musical was bringing me closer to the other kids, and I started to make more friends. Every night before I went to bed I'd rehearse my lines and songs until I knew them perfectly. I bubbled with excitement, thinking that this was the start of something really good.

A few weeks before the stage performance was to be held for the parents, I was doing my homework on the lounge floor as Kaley sat with a dummy in her mouth, watching the TV.

I had to draw a picture of a painting from one of our art textbooks and was so busy concentrating that I didn't see Kaley slip of the sofa and walk towards me. She bent down and pulled at the pages of my textbook.

'No, Kaley!' I pushed her away gently.

'I want,' she said, pulling the pages again until she ripped one out.

I put one hand over the book to stop her, pushing her away again with the other hand and she tripped and fell on her backside. A loud howling escaped from her mouth and she started bawling her eyes out.

Mum flew into the room, took one look at Kaley, and yelled, 'What have you done to her, you nasty little brat?'

'I haven't done anything, Mum. I was trying to stop her ripping up my book,' my voice came out shaky.

Mum kicked me in the ribs and picked up Kaley, cuddling her tight. 'What did that nasty brat do to you?' She smothered her with kisses, trying to calm her down, and disappeared off out of the room.

I knew I'd be in for it again so I tried to ignore the pain in my side and finish off my homework as quickly as possible while Kaley's screams filled the air.

Half an hour later, Mum stormed back in wearing a pair of Jim's heavy walking boots and stamped on my wrist so hard that I heard a loud crunching sound.

I yelled out in agony, rolling around on the floor, clutching my arm to my chest. I knew by the instant swelling and the bone jutting out at a funny angle that it was broken. The pain made my eyes water and I felt sick. Just looking at it brought on a fresh wave of nausea.

'Look what you made me do now!' she screamed. 'Why is it always you? I can't take much more of you. I wish you'd never been born.' A huge sigh escaped from her lips. 'Well, you can just wait until Kaley's feeling better before I take you to the hospital,' she sneered at me.

I thought I was going to pass out with the pain as I lay on the lounge floor, waiting until she could be bothered to get my wrist fixed. It seemed like forever before she came back, tied a tea towel around my arm in a makeshift sling, and made Kaley and me walk to the bus stop.

When we arrived at the hospital they asked Mum what happened and she told them I was climbing a tree in the garden and fell out. As Mum and Kaley stayed in the waiting room, a kind nurse led me back to the treatment room.

'Don't worry, pet, we'll fix you up really soon.' She gave me a huge smile. 'Take this painkiller and it'll help you feel much better.' She handed me a glass of water and a tablet that I knocked back.

I had an X-ray and then a doctor began setting my arm in a cast. 'It's not a bad break. You'll be back to normal in no time,' he said. 'But no climbing trees for a while, OK?'

I nodded glumly, biting my lip to stop myself blurting out what really happened.

As I left, the nurse handed me a lollypop. 'There you go, pet. That should cheer you up a bit.'

Mum ripped the lolly out of my hand on the way home and gave it to Kaley.

'Well, there's no way you're going to be doing Grease now, is there?' She grinned at me. 'I'll write the school a letter and say you can't perform with a broken wrist.' There was a glint of triumph in her eyes.

I didn't give her the satisfaction of letting her know how upset I was, but that night I wept uncontrollably as I tried to get to sleep through the pain. I wasn't sure how much more I could take. It wasn't just my arm that was broken. Inside I was broken too. I had to find a way out.

# CHAPTER 14

The following week, I returned to school with a sense of determination. I couldn't carry on letting Mum do this to me. If something didn't happen soon, I really would go crazy, and I was worried that she would either permanently disable me, or worse, she'd kill me.

Although she'd always drummed into me not to tell anyone, I'd reached a mental breaking point. I had to tell someone. What was the alternative? Stay there until I could legally leave home at sixteen, which meant another four years of abuse? I couldn't take anymore.

I'd always been a star pupil at school. I had little else in my life to keep me occupied, and it was the only place I could escape to that gave me some respite. It was also practically the only area of my life that I had control over. I always thought deep down that education might be my way to escape Mum for good eventually. If I studied hard and got a good job in the future, I could turn my back on her forever. And the memories of being called a thief from my old school permanently haunted me. I didn't want to draw any unwanted and negative attention to myself at school so I was always on my best behaviour. I had enough unwanted attention at home.

I never knew what happened to Nan and Aunty Linda. I didn't know where they were. I had no address or phone number, so I couldn't contact them to try and help me. The only other option was someone at school. My drama teacher Mr Hyde was always kind to me, and when we were rehearsing for the Grease musical, I got to know him a bit better and felt very comfortable with him. Sometimes I'd catch him glancing at me with a look of sympathy, and I wondered if he knew what was going on at home. How could he not know? I was black and blue half the time. But in those days, no one seemed to do anything about child abuse. I knew Amy's parents didn't hit her or her brothers and sisters, but there were a few boys in the class who I'd overhear talking about how their dad gave them a belting now and then or their mum smacked their bottoms. If it was going on everywhere, maybe it really was normal.

I wanted to ask Mr Hyde's advice about what I should do, but it was hard to pluck up the courage. After Mum broke my arm, I'd been rehearsing in my mind what I could say. There were so many things that had gone on over the years, I'd forgotten a lot of it, and however I thought about starting the conversation it never seemed right. How did a twelve-year-old explain the cycle of abuse, the isolation, all her sick and twisted punishments, the madness and destruction? She threatened many times over that if I told, no one would believe me. What if he thought I was a liar?

'Don't waste your breath telling anyone,' Mum said more times than I can count. 'Who's going to believe a little brat like you?' She glanced down at her immaculate clothes and her perfect hair and nails. 'Look at me,' she mocked, then pointed a finger at my hair that had grown into a messy bob after she'd hacked it, my skinny frame, and my bruises and scars of varying shades. 'And look at you. Why would they believe a piece of rubbish like you? They'll think you're a liar.'

Memories of being called a thief and a liar at school drifted into my head.

'They'll wonder why you've kept quiet all this time and never said anything before. If I'm so bad, you would've told someone, wouldn't you?' She gave me a self-satisfied smile.

And I believed her. She was very good at acting like the perfect mum whenever we were in public. She could've won an Oscar for her performances and was always plausible and convincing. Who would believe me? I'd been brainwashed into believing that everything she did to me was all my fault.

Another favourite threat of hers was, 'Even if they do try and take you away from me, where do you think you'll end up? A home for unwanted children, that's where. And do you want to know what they do to the brats there?' She'd raise an eyebrow and sneer at me. 'They'll kick the shit out of you so much you'll be begging to come back home. Do you think they like looking after those useless brats that no one wants?' She'd get close in my face and sneer at me. 'You've got it easy here. It's nothing compared to those children's homes. If they take you away, everyone will know what a horrible, naughty little brat you are and they'll blame you. Everyone will hate you.' Then she'd use her trump card. 'And you'll be responsible for Kaley being taken away, too. Can you live with that on your conscience?'

And I feared she was right. My home life might've been filled with unbelievable horrors, but if I was taken away by strangers who hated me, too, surely I could suffer even more abuse. How could I be responsible for Kaley being removed into a place like that as well? It would be all my fault if she was taken away. I couldn't live with myself if that happened.

Then she'd try another strategy just to drum it in more. 'Anyway, it's not like they can do anything. It's completely legal to give your kids physical punishment. If you were better behaved, I wouldn't have to do it.' A smug smile settled on her face.

So I was incredibly worried about approaching My Hyde. Negative thoughts whirled around in my head: *What if he wouldn't do anything anyway and I just got it worse when she found out. What if they all thought I was a liar and wouldn't believe me? What if they did take me to a children's home and I get more abuse?*

Then the positive thoughts took over: *You have to DO something. You can't go on like this. Don't be a baby and tell them everything!*

I forced down the anxiety inside as the possibility of getting away from her spurred me on, and I waited for the next drama class to take my chance. I wanted to catch My Hyde after class when all the other kids had left for lunch break, and I could barely contain myself during the two hour lesson. Usually I lapped up his instructions and threw myself into whatever role we had to play, but that day I couldn't concentrate on anything. I fluffed my lines, getting all tongue-tied, and I didn't answer when someone spoke to me. When My Hyde asked us all to mime feelings of happiness, I just froze. It seemed so ironic. Happiness? What was that?

Half way through the lesson, Lee, one of the naughtier boys in our class who was always getting in trouble, began unzipping a few of the girls' skirts without them noticing. A girl called Tania screamed suddenly and everyone turned to look at her. Her skirt had slipped to the floor and she desperately tried to do it back up, hiccupping with tears. Another girl called Lindsay was doing the same.

Mr Hyde marched to the front of the class, his face red and contorted with anger. 'Who did this?' he yelled at everyone, making them jump.

One of the other girls pointed at Lee. 'He did, sir. He tried to do it to me, too.'

My Hyde yanked Lee by his arm and dragged him out into the corridor, slamming the door to the drama studio.

'Bend over!' we heard Mr Hyde shout, closely followed by a crack of the cane hitting poor Lee's bottom. I knew Lee shouldn't have done it, but it seemed so overboard to cane him for something like that.

It made me jump with fright every time there was another crack or scream from Lee. Although corporal punishment in schools was rife at that time, I'd never seen Mr Hyde act like that. Some of the other teachers would regularly cane people or give them the slipper. My Hyde had lost his temper a few times and given people detentions, but I never saw him dish out any kind of physical punishment.

A lump formed in my throat, rendering me speechless, and silent tears threatened to choke me. My sadness seemed to swallow me whole. If the teachers were at it, too, what chance did I have? Mr Hyde had been my only hope, and he would never help me now if he sanctioned that kind of punishment.

# CHAPTER 15

I sunk further and further into despair. There would be no escape for me. As my thirteenth birthday rolled around, I did finally have something to look forward to, though. The school had organized a week long trip to Cuffley Camp, an outdoor centre in the middle of huge woods with lots of educational and fun activities to keep us occupied. I nearly wet myself with excitement as we were told what kind of things they had on offer there. Cycling, abseiling, nature walks, assault courses, archery, and much more. It would be the first time I'd ever had a holiday and been away from Mum and I couldn't wait. I was amazed that she'd actually let me go, but I think it was more Jim's influence. He'd been complaining a lot to Mum recently that he never got any peace when he came home at the weekends because of her constant screaming at me, and I think he wanted some time when I wasn't around. That suited me just fine! We had to take our own equipment like sleeping bags, toiletries, plastic cutlery and plates, torches, and pillows. I was worried how the other kids would look at me when I wasn't dressed in my school uniform. I was never allowed the latest fashions like them and had very few clothes that weren't threadbare or faded. I was so grateful when Jim came home one weekend with a sleeping bag and a pair of new jeans and a jumper for me that I threw my arms around his neck and hugged him. My depression instantly lifted, and for once, I was the happiest girl in the world.

Amy and I had it all planned. We would be sharing a tent with two other girls, Emily and Clare. Amy's parents would give her enough treats so we could have a midnight feast on our first night. Finally, I was being allowed my first taste of freedom like normal kids. I tried not to show my increasing excitement around Mum because I knew she'd find some way of stopping me from going if she felt like it.

We were a rowdy, giggling mass as we piled onto a coach one Friday morning at school. The other parents were all there to wave goodbye to their kids. Everyone except my mum, of course.

When we arrived at the camp, we had our own 'village,' which had tents already set up on the edge of the woods. In front of the tents were a camp fire, a covered area that had a long wooden table and bench chairs for us to eat, and a barbeque. At the edge of the tents there was a bigger tent that would be used for preparing the food. There was a rota for which kids would help with the cooking. Since I was used to cooking dinners for Mum at an early age, I volunteered to go first, and my job was peeling piles of potatoes so we could have sausages, mash, and beans on the first night.

We were given a timetable of our daily activities,

but I was especially looking forward to the wood scramble, nature walks, pond dipping, bug hunts, and abseiling. I spent most of my life cooped up in that house so anything that involved being outdoors was like heaven to me. Since I'd never owned a bike, cycling was low down on my list of things that I wanted to do, but I was adamant that I'd try everything they had to offer.

The teachers told us we had to make our own beds out of straw and pointed to a big pile of dry straw next to the eating area. They showed us how to fill big plastic covers with the straw to use as a mattress, but however much I tried to get it smooth and comfy, mine always ended up lumpy. Still, sleeping on a lumpy bed was a small price to pay.

After we'd set up our beds, it was time for orienteering and we all filed off for a walk around the camp and woods. Next, we had to build a shelter out of logs and rope and canvas, and then it was lunch time. I helped the teachers prepare cheese sandwiches and we all ate at the long table before an afternoon of more activities like archery and rounders. After I'd helped with the dinner, we sat around the camp fire singing songs.

When it was time to go to bed, Amy, Clare, Emily, and I made up ghost stories in our tent after lights out, shining a torch under our faces so it gave off an eerie glow until they got scared and wanted to stop. Nothing they made up could scare me, though. I'd seen far more scarier things at home. We were too tired to have our midnight feast that night and we all fell into a deep sleep on our lumpy mattresses. The next morning we were awoken by the teachers banging on the tent posts, waking us up for a breakfast of beans on toast. Because I was still suffering from anorexia, I pushed my food around my plate while the others tucked in with glee.

We had plenty of free time, too, and I'd spend hours playing bat and ball, Frisbee, or football with Amy and the others. It was so much fun I never wanted it to end. I even tried the cycling with the other kids. They made it look so easy, how difficult could it be? With nervous excitement and encouragement from Amy, I climbed aboard one of the bikes. After a few minutes of Amy supporting me as I spun the peddles, I was off, the wheels wobbling precariously until I'd managed to find my balance and learnt how to steer. I took a few tumbles but it was well worth it.

On the second day we were there, the teachers told us we had to have showers, so we all got our wash bags and trundled off to the shower block for a cold shower. There was a bench along one of the walls with hooks for us to leave our clothes, and because I was having such a good time, I completely forgot about hiding my scarred body from the others. As I happily stripped off, I turned around to see Amy and some of the other kids staring at my naked skin with their mouths wide open. Over the years, I'd become so adept at hiding my scars from others. If we had gym class, I'd wear long sleeve tops and tracksuit bottoms and change in the toilets instead of the communal changing rooms. None of them had ever seen the full extent of what Mum did to me before.

Embarrassed, I quickly ran into the shower,

wanting to get it over with as quickly as possible so I could put some clean clothes on and cover up once more. By the time I was dressed, the others were still in the showers so I ran back to the camp as quickly as I could and sat alone in my tent, feeling like a freak. During the last two days, Clare and Emily had shared stories of their parents and their brothers and sisters. How they would go on family outings; how their parents looked after them; how they always had the latest gadgets and toys. I already knew Amy's parents were lovely to her, too. They'd showed me a whole new world, one where parents loved their kids, showered them with praise and kisses and gifts. A world where their parents nurtured and looked after them. A world where the parents thrived on their own joy of seeing their child happy and contented. Now I felt like the 'weird' kid again. Instead of pretending to be just like them, now they'd know that I was different and then they'd surely start to wonder why my Mum was like that. Would they blame me? Would they whisper and snigger about me behind my back? Would they think I was so horrible that I deserved what my mum did to me?

I lay back on my mattress, dreading them coming back, feeling sick to my stomach. It wasn't long before Amy was at the entrance, biting her lip with a look of hesitation.

'Can I come in?' she asked.

I sat up, worried that she was going to tell me she didn't want to be my friend anymore. 'Of course. It's your tent, too.' I laughed, trying to make light of the situation.

She sat down, cross-legged on my mattress. 'Doesn't your Mum help you when your stepdad does this?'

I let out a bitter laugh. 'It's her that's caused most of it.'

'Do you want to talk about it?'

So I did. For the first time in my life, I did tell someone. I poured my heart out to my best friend, and it felt so good to finally get it off my chest. I didn't tell her everything that had happened but I told her the most horrible things that had a huge effect on me. I even surprised myself by recounting the years without crying. I think I was way past tears at that stage. I was just numb with it all. Amy cried enough tears for me, and strangely, it was me that ended up comforting her.

'But it's wrong,' she said, wiping away her tears with the heel of her hand. 'My mum and dad never do anything like that to us.'

I shrugged. 'What can I do about it?' I said, but for the first time in my life I was absolutely sure it was wrong. This wasn't normal behaviour for my mum to be doing these things to me.

'She shouldn't be able to get away with it,' Amy said.

'I know, but there's no one to help me.'

Her eyes flashed suddenly with an idea. 'Why don't you run away? You could come and live with me and my family.'

'I'd love to, Amy, but Mum would find me straight away and bring me back.'

'So, where else could you go?'

'I don't know. I don't know where my nan and

aunty are, and even if I found them, Mum would probably drag me straight back. I don't want to end up in a children's home, either, it might be even worse. And if I tell someone, they'll take Kaley away, too, and I couldn't bear for her to be abused on one of those places.'

During the rest of the week at camp, Amy and I would sneak off and talk about what I could do or where I could go. The thought of running away to London and living on the streets was preferable to going home. Surely, it couldn't be any worse than the way I was living already, but I was twelve years old, how would I get money for food? Where would I sleep? What if I was attacked?

When the day finally came for us to leave the camp, I dreaded going back home. As the coach dropped us off at the school gates, I hugged Amy goodbye and she ran off to her mum and dad who were waiting with a beaming smile on their faces. I watched as she threw herself into their arms. The look of pure happiness radiating from all of them twisted a knife of jealousy in my stomach. I wanted that too.

I walked home slowly, trying to delay the inevitable. I'd had a week of freedom and now I was returning to my torturous prison.

I slid my key in the lock, took a deep breath, and turned. The house was silent when I went in. I was making my way up the stairs when Mum flew out of the lounge, grabbing me by my shirt collar and pulling me back down the stairs. Since I'd been away, she had no one to take her anger out on because she would never touch Kaley. Now I'd be getting the full force of it.

'Had a good time, did you?' she glared at me.

I stood in front of her, glaring back. Suddenly, I felt braver. Maybe it was all the talk of running away, or the fact that I'd spent the past week living like a normal kid that made me defiant. From that moment on, there was no way I was going to show her that I was scared of her.

'Yes, it was really nice, thank you,' I said.

Her eyes widened with surprise at the fact that I'd answered her without cowering or pleading with her, and she gripped my collar tighter.

'Really?' she said in a sarcastic tone, tilting her head. 'And what sort of *nice* things did you do?'

'Nature walks, bug hunting, cycling–'

I didn't get any further than that. She cut me off with a punch to the side of the head, sending my face catapulting to the side.

'Don't you answer me back, you bitch! Don't you dare answer me back,' she screamed, pulling me into the kitchen.

She grabbed a broom that was already propped up against the kitchen table, ready and waiting for me.

'I'm not having any of your cheek.' She whacked me over and over again on my back, my arms, my head.

Instinctively, I assumed the survival position, crouching down on the floor and trying to protect my head with my hands

Roughly, she pulled at my hands, her blows reigning down on me over and over again as she yelled obscenities. When she was out of breath and worn out she threw the broom at me and stormed

111

out of the room, leaving me to crawl to my bedroom.

Welcome home.

The serpent of depression and loneliness reared its ugly head as it clutched at my insides, building momentum, squeezing tighter and tighter until I felt I was suffocated from it all. Even my schoolwork held no pleasure for me now. The newfound braveness that I'd felt on returning from camp quickly diminished with the realisation that my dreams of escape would never come true. I had nowhere to go.

Life carried on in a round of terror and pain, and it would take another year before I finally managed to get free.

# CHAPTER 16

I was surprised one day when Jim was waiting for me at home after school instead of Mum. His face was wrinkled in a worried frown, and Kaley sat on his knee, reading a book quietly.

Kaley looked up and jumped off his knee when she saw me, running into my stomach for a hug. 'Hello Bat,' she said, which was her nickname for me. She'd got so used to Mum calling me Brat and never using my real name, Kaley always copied her but she could never pronounce the R properly.

'Guess where Mummy is?' Kaley asked me.

'I don't know,' I said warily.

'She's in the hopital,' Kaley said.

'You mean hospital?' I picked her up and gave her a cuddle.

'She was rushed to hospital with appendicitis,' Jim said, rubbing at his forehead.

*Yes! I hope she dies and puts me out of my misery.*

It was a cruel thought, but that's how I felt. I hoped she was in as much pain as she'd given me for such a long time. I know that some victims of abuse still love their abusers, but I'd long since stopped feeling love for her. I hated her with a passion for everything she'd done to me. In my mind a glimpse of a new happy life came into view. A life that didn't include her, where I was loved and cherished and protected.

'Will she be OK?' I asked.

He nodded, running a hand through his thinning hair. 'Yes. I have to go back to the hospital this afternoon for visiting hours and she should be out of recovery.'

The fleeting glimpse of any new life disappeared from view.

Since we didn't have a phone still, Jim couldn't ring them to find out if she was all right, but all afternoon as I did my chores and homework and cooked dinner for him and Kaley, I harboured secret hopes that she wouldn't wake up from the anesthetic.

He left that afternoon to go and see her and came back with news. Bad for me. Good for her. The operation went well and she was fine. She'd be back home again in seven days.

I disappeared to my room and punched my mattress, crying into my pillow. Here was my one chance for escape her forever and fate hadn't stepped in to save me. But fate did have one ace up its sleeve. Because Mum wasn't there and Jim was out visiting her, I had more time to myself. I didn't dare go out and play in case he came home early, but it did give me the opportunity to search through Mum's drawers and cupboards to see if I could find an address or phone number for Nan or Linda. Ever since Cuffley Camp, plans of running away were the first thing I thought of when I woke up in the morning and the last thing that went through my head at night.

I settled Kaley down in front of the TV watching Play School, her favourite show, and crept into Mum and Jim's bedroom. I searched through boxes and boxes of shoes, looked in pockets, in drawers, ran my hand along the top shelves, hoping to find a scrap of paper that would tell me what I needed to know. Before Jim came back that night I abandoned my search and did my homework. I'd waited ten years since Mum came to get me. I could wait another day to carry on.

On the third day of searching I got lucky. Hidden under a loose floorboard in their room was a battered shoe box. Inside was an old address book and photos of my Dad, Geoff. I picked them up, replacing the floorboard just as it had been, and took it into my bedroom, hiding it under my bed so I could inspect it under the cover of darkness when everyone had gone to bed because I couldn't risk Kaley catching me and telling Mum what I was up to.

It seemed to take forever until bed time arrived. I gnawed on my fingernails with anticipation, wondering if Nan or Linda's address was hidden in that little black book.

'Stop fidgeting!' Jim slapped my hands away and scowled at me as he watched TV.

'Sorry,' I mumbled, trying to concentrate on the screen but not hearing a word.

Finally, I sloped off to bed, shut the door, and turned off the light.

Using the torch that I'd borrowed from Jim to take to Cuffley Camp, I opened the address book.

Flicking straight through to the page for the letter L, I ran a fingertip down it, my gaze desperately searching out Linda's name.

It wasn't there.

Tears pricked at my eyes.

I should've realized that her address wouldn't be there. Mum had cut off ties with Linda when I moved in with her, and after Nan's only visit to me, Mum had moved us all away so they couldn't find us. What kind of a person did that to such loving people as Nan and Linda?

Then I had a sudden thought. Maybe Mum hadn't written her address under L for Linda's first name. Maybe it was under her surname.

One by one, I turned the pages, scouring each and every one. When I reached the letter M I found the word *Mother* along with an address and phone number scrawled in Mum's messy handwriting.

My heart did an excited tap dance in my chest as I continued looking for Linda's details. Her address and phone number were listed under P for Parker.

I punched my arm in the air in celebration. This was going to be my escape.

I copied out the addresses and phone numbers carefully onto a piece of paper, checking and double checking them numerous times. I only had once chance to get this right. When Mum came home, there was no way I'd be able to sneak in her room again without getting caught.

When I was finally satisfied I'd copied everything correctly, I quickly stuffed it into a text book and hid it at the bottom of my school bag. Then I turned my attention to the photos of my Dad.

I really looked like him. I had his dark wavy hair and the same shaped brown eyes. The first time I remembered meeting Mum at Nan's house she seemed so annoyed that I looked like my Dad, and over the years she would constantly berate him, saying how he'd left her all alone, and that he didn't really love her because he went and died. In her mind I think she really believed that it was either his fault he got killed in a car accident, selfishly leaving her with a young daughter to look after, or my fault because she gave birth to me. Only she didn't look after me. She palmed me off on Nan and had a breakdown, and then after that she couldn't have cared less about me. I knew she hated me because I reminded her so much of him and she blamed me for him dying.

In every photo he was smiling happily for the camera, showing off perfectly white teeth. In the photos of him and Mum together with their arms wrapped around each other, she looked relaxed and happy, joining in with his wide smile. She looked nothing like the crazy, deranged woman who put me through hell.

I kept one photo of Dad and stuffed it in a textbook as well. The next day, when Jim was at the hospital, I snuck the box back under the floorboards exactly how I'd found it, carefully making sure there were no telltale signs that it had been disturbed.

Now I would bide my time. No matter what happened. I would escape.

# CHAPTER 17

I only had a small window of opportunity while Mum was in hospital because as soon as she got out she would be monitoring my every move as usual. She knew exactly how long it took to get the school bus home, and if I was even ten minutes late, she would fly into a rage, screaming and punching me for defying her. She wanted my world to be total isolation.

The morning after I discovered the phone numbers I awoke for the first time with a new emotion. Hope. All I had to do was phone Nan or Linda and I felt sure they would know what to do. They would save me from my nightmare.

I was never allowed pocket money and Mum always obsessively counted everything in her purse to ensure I wouldn't be able to slip in there unnoticed and steal money to buy something without her permission. In the ambulance's rush to take her to the hospital, Mum's handbag was still in a drawer in the kitchen, but there was no way I could steal money in case she found out. I would have to try and steal if from Jim instead.

Whenever I did my chores of washing clothes I checked the pockets for pieces of tissue and change.

Jim had a habit of leaving sweet wrappers and tissues in his trouser pockets, and if I neglected my duties of removing them and they broke down in the washing machine, covering the black clothes with blobs of white fluff, Mum would go mad. For the next few days, I checked his pockets with mounting anticipation. All I needed was a few ten pence pieces and I could call the family I desperately missed. Every day I was rewarded with only the usual used tissues.

On the fifth day after she was admitted, I told Amy my plan and asked if she could lend me some change for the phone box. As good a friend as she was, she came up trumps.

'I asked my mum if I could have some extra dinner money today.' Amy beamed at me as she met me on the school bus. 'Here.' She handed me some change and I stuffed it in my pocket. It may have only been a few coins but they now became my lifeline. With tears in her eyes, she said, 'Good luck. If you go to stay with your Nan or Linda, I'm going to really miss you.' She gave me a huge hug and I clutched onto her.

'I'm never going to forget you,' I said as we bumped along the road to school.

There was a phone box in the village I lived in but I couldn't risk calling before school in case Jim saw me or I missed the bus. I would have to do it after school since he didn't know the exact time the school bus dropped me back off.

The day passed with painful slowness. Every time I glanced nervously at the clock, the hands had only turned a few minutes. It took all my willpower just to try and sit still. I was so close to ending my nightmare, and the butterflies in my stomach, coupled with the anorexia and lack of food made me heady. The room swam around me as I struggled to concentrate on my lessons.

Finally, the day ended and I caught the bus back to the village. As Amy waved me off, she gave me another tight hug and wished me luck again. I waited for the bus to drive off and instead of heading home, I went in the other direction and hurried to the phone box.

I scrambled in my bag, looking for the book I'd hidden the piece of paper in.

I searched through the pages but couldn't find it.

With a rising sense of panic, tears pricked at my eyes as I turned the book upside down and fluttered the pages, shaking the book hard, but nothing fell out.

I knew this was the book. It had to be in there. It just had to be.

*Calm down! It's in there somewhere. I know it is.*

As hysteria shook my whole body, I pulled out each book, one by one, and began searching the pages. When I finished an overwhelming feeling of dread overcame me. The piece of paper had disappeared.

I peered into the bottom of my now empty bag but my streaming tears blurred my vision. Quickly wiping my eyes on my shoulders, I finally saw it. It must've fallen out of the book and wormed its way to the bottom of my bag.

I snatched it out, unfolded it, and picked up the phone. I was in such a state of distress it took a few goes of punching in Nan's phone number before I finally got it right.

An automated voice said, 'The number you have dialed is incorrect. Please replace the handset and try again.'

My eyes widened. I was sure I'd got the number right. I tried again and got the same message.

My heart sunk to my stomach. For some reason Nan's phone number was wrong. Had she been disconnected? Had she moved to another house with a different number?

I tried Linda's number and listened to the phone ringing and ringing with no answer. Finally, the phone cut me off.

I stared at the handset. *This can't be happening. Please tell me this isn't happening.*

I tried again but it was the same. No answer.

I slammed the receiver down, gathered up my books, and walked home with heavy legs. I had two days left to try again before Mum was released from the hospital.

The next day, I repeated my exercise, growing increasingly nauseas as I waited for every second of the day to pass. I tried Jenny's number again after school but there was still no answer.

That afternoon and evening I carried out my chores on autopilot while Jim was at the hospital visiting Mum. I ironed the bed sheets and clothes, I made Kaley's dinner, I dusted and vacuumed the house, I did my homework, all the while praying for something or someone to help me.

When Jim returned that night he had a grave expression on his face.

'What's happened?' I asked, hoping that my praying had resulted in Mum taking a turn for the worse. I bit my lip, waiting for his answer.

'Your mum's scar where they removed her appendix isn't healing properly. They want to keep her in for a few more days,' he said wearily.

I could've kissed him or punched the air with relief.

Instead, I said, 'Oh, that's terrible.' I turned away to make him a sandwich with a smile of immense relief on my face.

The following day I was back in the phone box again after school, dialling Linda's number.

*Please be in. Please be in. Please help me.*

It rang a few times and then a voice said, 'Hello?' It was a voice I recognized from my childhood. A voice that filled me with such pure joy that I immediately started crying.

'Hello? Who is this?' Linda asked.

Through my sniffles and cries I managed to answer, 'It's Sarah, Aunty Linda.'

I heard her take a sharp breath in. 'Oh, my. Sarah? Is that really you?'

I leant against the side of the phone box for support, afraid that my legs would give way and I'd flop to the floor.

'We've been so worried about you. Where are you? What happened to you? We've been trying to find you all these years,' she gushed.

'We live in a village in Bedfordshire now. I tried to phone Nan but the number must be wrong.'

She paused for a second. 'I'm so sorry, Sarah, she's gone. She died a few years ago.'

I felt like the world had collapsed from underneath me. The loving woman who had taken care of me for the first four years of my life had gone and I didn't even have the chance to say goodbye. I tried to picture her face again but I couldn't. It had been so long since I'd been deprived of seeing her. A lump rose in my throat as memories of her unconditional love flew into my mind. How she'd played with me, fussed over me, built sandcastles for hours with me. The cuddles she lavished on me, and the scent of her Lily of the Valley perfume on her skin as she kissed me. It was too much to bear.

'No,' I wailed, sobbing uncontrollably.

Through my animal sounds of grief, I heard Linda's voice filtering through to me.

'We never knew where you went. I'm so sorry, Sarah. What happened to you? Are you all right?'

I took deep breaths and began to tell her but I heard a beeping sound in my ear, signalling the end of my money.

'My money's running out!' I yelled, panicking.

'Sarah, phone the operator and reverse the charges,' Linda said in a calm voice.

I took a deep breath and did as she said, finally being reconnected with her. Slowly, I recounted the years of abuse. The punches, the kicks, the choking, the cigarette burns, the isolation, the neglect, the fear, and the pain. There was so much to say and so little time.

She listened, occasionally interrupting me, with gasps of horror and questions.

'What's your address?' she asked. 'We'll drive up

and get you. I'm not leaving you there for a minute longer.'

I gave her the address.

'Go home and get your belongings together but don't let on what's happening,' Linda said. 'It'll take us a few hours to get there. I love you, sweetheart.'

Those four words almost cracked my heart into a million pieces. I'd been wanting to hear them all these years from Mum instead of all the taunts, ridicule, threats, and vile mental abuse.

'I love you too, Aunty Linda,' I choked.

# CHAPTER 18

I ran all the way home, out of breath and weak when I arrived. Jim had taken Kaley to the hospital with him that day so the house was empty.

I looked at the clock in the kitchen. Four-thirty p.m. Visiting hours ended at seven p.m. so I had plenty of time to pack my meagre belongings before they arrived. With any luck, Linda and Clive would get here before Jim and Kaley returned.

I didn't have many clothes or toys. Even though I was fifteen, I still slept with my original stuffed cat Dusty for company. He was threadbare now – one of his ears had long since fallen off and one of the buttons for his eyes was missing – but he was the only reminder I had of Nan.

I held Dusty to my chest, choking up again as I thought of the kind old lady with white hair and an apron around her waist who loved me with a passion and thought I was her little princess. Where had that child gone? The child she loved so much? She'd been systematically beaten into oblivion. In her place was a neglected bone-thin child with an eating disorder. A child who had little confidence or self-esteem. A child who'd tried to end her life to get away from it all. A child who avoided her

125

reflection in the mirror because when she dared to look, all she could see were haunting eyes with dark circles underneath that told a story of sadness. She saw someone she hated and wasn't worthy of love. A child who hardly ever smiled because she had very little to smile about. Would Linda and her family see that too? Or would they look beyond that to the girl they once loved and welcome me with open arms?

I heard Jim's key in the lock and my back stiffened. I sat in front of the TV, trying to concentrate on the screen but not hearing or seeing anything. All I could think about was Linda coming.

'Make us a sandwich,' Jim shouted to me, slapping me over the head. 'You lazy cow. Haven't you got chores you should be doing instead of lounging around watching the television?'

'I've finished them,' I mumbled, getting off the sofa and rushing to make him and Kaley a sandwich.

Kaley babbled about how excited she was that Mum would be coming home in a few days, and I half-listened to her, nodding and agreeing with her while my mind was focused on only one thing.

At eight-thirty p.m. there was a knock on the door and I braced myself for what was to come. I followed Jim along the hall, excitedly waiting for the first glimpse of my aunt.

As he swung the door open, Linda and Clive burst in. 'Where is she? Where's Sarah?'

Jim stood with his mouth agape. 'Who the hell are you?'

Linda saw me hovering in the hallway and held

126

out her arms. I ran into them and she enveloped me in a warm hug, showering my face with kisses.

I was vaguely aware of Jim and Clive having a heated discussion with angry voices and arms flying around, but I didn't have a clue what they were saying, I was too busy soaking up Linda's love.

Kaley wandered into the hall, her eyes wide, watching with surprise. She showed no fear at the shouting, having been used to seeing Mum and Jim's anger being directed at me. She was six years old and had developed a nervous twitch in her right eye whenever she spoke. I think it was how her fragile mind dealt with witnessing my abuse on a daily basis. Although she was never subjected to it herself, we loved each other deeply, and even if she couldn't explain it or voice her emotions to Mum, she couldn't help but feel my pain throughout the years. My only regret at leaving would be saying goodbye to her.

Linda released her tight grip on me, clutching my face in her hands as she studied me with shock. 'I'm so sorry,' she repeated over again. 'I failed you. None of this is your fault, Sarah.' The kindness in her voice made tears rush to the surface, spilling out onto my cheeks. She hugged me close for a while. Finally, she stood and said, 'Go and get your things.'

I ran into my room and collected them. When I came out, Linda was glaring at Jim who wouldn't look at her. I saw an unexpected expression on his face that I'd never seen before – shame.

'How could you do this to a child?' Linda spat at him. 'Don't you have any conscience?'

'You should be locked up forever.' Geoff picked up my small plastic bags and pushed past Jim, leaving him standing there with his mouth open.

I knelt down in front of Kaley.

'I have to leave,' I said to her. 'I'm so sorry, but I can't stay here anymore.'

She threw her arms around my neck.

'Please don't go. I'll miss you.' She wept.

I hugged her tighter. 'I'll miss you, too.'

'Come on. We need to go,' Linda said gently.

'I'll write to you, Kaley.' And with a final hug, Linda took my hand and led me outside.

I couldn't even look at Jim as I left.

I slid onto the backseat of their car, waving at Kaley who stood crying and confused on the doorstep. I waved at her until the car turned a corner and she slipped out of my sight forever.

I was about to start a new chapter in my life.

# CHAPTER 19

'Are you hungry?' Linda swivelled around in the front seat of the car and smiled at me.

For the first time in a long time, I was. I nodded, grinning back at her because I couldn't speak. The unfurling of immense relief had made my tongue silent.

We stopped at a motorway service station where I managed to eat half a cheeseburger.

A frown of concern passed between Linda and Clive.

'You're not eating very much,' Linda said to me. 'You're so thin, you need to eat something.'

After all the time of practically being starved and later starving myself, my stomach had shrunk so much that I could only manage small amounts at once.

'I'm so full up,' I said.

She reached out and squeezed my hand, not wanting to push me further.

On the final leg of my journey I fell into an exhausted sleep. The anxiety and fear of the last few days had taken their toll, not to mention the last eleven years.

In the darkness, I was being awoken by Linda.

'Wake up sleepy head, we're here.' She ruffled my hair.

I gazed out the car window and rubbed my eyes. 'You moved house.'

Linda nodded. 'Yes, a couple of years ago. It's a good job we kept the same phone number or you wouldn't have found us.' She gave me a huge smile. 'Come on, let's get you inside.'

Beth, who was now seventeen, ran out of the front door and down the path to greet me.

'Oh, my God, I can't believe that last time I saw you was so long ago.' Beth flung her arms around me. 'I'm so glad you're here. You're going to be sharing a room with me, and if you need to borrow any clothes or stuff, just help yourself, OK?' she babbled with excitement.

I nodded back, smiling but dumbstruck at the show of generosity from people who were now virtual strangers.

'Come on,' she pulled me into the house. 'Let me show you my room.'

As I followed her up the stairs, I took in the smells of home-cooked meals, the family photos on the wall, the warmth of the central heating. This was a proper home, not just a house.

'Wow,' I said, looking around her room. It was painted in pale pink colours with all the nick-nacks of a young woman dotted around. Makeup and perfume bottles on a white dressing table, cupboards bursting with clothes, shoes and handbags, books and games on nearby shelves. 'This is lovely!'

Next to her bed with a purple and pink duvet and

matching pillows there was a mattress placed on the floor made up for me.

'Do you want me to curl your hair? I've been practicing on mine. I can make it look really pretty,' she asked, staring at my long dark hair that hadn't been cut since Mum had butchered it with the kitchen scissors.

'Yes, please.' I nodded eagerly.

It was the start of a firm friendship that would fill me with happiness. I didn't meet Jane until the next day because she'd been out with her boyfriend the night before, but she, too, welcomed me into their family with kindness and caring.

No one spoke about what had happened to me at first. Linda refused to press me, probably realising that I would talk about things in my own time. Instead, they lavished me with food, clothes, attention, and trips out. I had entered a new world of being protected and cherished that I'd only glimpsed from the outside since leaving Nan.

Beth took charge of showing me around the area, revelling in her new role as big sister. Some of my fondest memories are walking along Bournemouth pier at the weekends or shopping with Beth, and visiting Weymouth and Chesil beach that invoked strong feelings of Nan. Somehow, I sensed she was watching down on me and smiling. Beth took me to Nan's grave, and as I knelt down in front of her head stone, a rush of love and sadness threatened to overwhelm me. I placed some flowers I'd bought on her grave, chatting to her about how good things would be from now on and telling her how much I'd missed her. Finally, I got to say my goodbyes to the kind lady who loved me unconditionally, but the loss of her still leaves a mark on my heart.

About a week after I arrived, Beth and I came home one day to find Linda, flushed with anger, screaming down the phone.

'You're crazy!' she yelled into the receiver. 'No, you're not coming to get her. If you go anywhere near her again, I'll report both of you to the police. Call yourself a mother? You're not fit to look after a dog! I've seen the scars on her body. You're evil!' She slammed the phone down.

I glanced at Beth nervously, feeling bad for causing so much trouble, then I suddenly burst into tears as a whole mixture of feelings hit me: relief, happiness, sadness, anger, guilt.

Linda took a deep breath and hugged me. 'Sorry you had to hear that.'

'She won't be able to take me away, will she?' I asked.

'Come into the kitchen. We need to have a talk,' she said.

Beth disappeared upstairs giving me an encouraging smile as I followed Linda into the kitchen. She made us both a steaming mug of hot chocolate before she sat down opposite me.

'Because you're still fifteen, you're not legally allowed to leave home,' she started.

I sucked in a sharp gasp of breath as her words swam in my ears. Would she send me back?

'But, there's no way I'm going to let her take you back. Not after what she's done to you. If she tries to take you back I'll go to court and fight her if I have to. It's not right. Everything she did isn't right.'

Once again, I felt an amazing gratitude towards her. 'I don't know how to thank you.' I hugged her tight.

'You don't need to thank me,' she sniffed, her eyes clouding with emotion. 'How can I have such a monster for a sister?'

Mum never rang again and the police were never called to report me missing so I assumed that she just accepted the fact I was gone. It wasn't like she was going to miss me, after all. I phoned Amy regularly and she told me Mum, Jim, and Kaley had moved out of the village shortly after the phone call she'd had with Linda. I had no idea where they'd gone.

Beth was in the sixth form and I was quickly enrolled in the same school as her. The other kids in my class were intrigued by my different accent and I made friends pretty much straight away. Because I'd always thrown myself into schoolwork, I was put into the top sets for my classes, mixing with other kids who had a real drive to learn. When I was younger I'd dreamt of going to university, and ever since I'd discovered my love of animals, I knew I wanted to be a vet, but university was expensive. Linda and Clive weren't poor but they weren't well off, either, and now they had an unexpected mouth to feed so I didn't think I'd be realising my ambition.

I got a paper round to try and contribute in some small way, even though they told me I didn't need to, and I offered them all of my weekly pay in exchange for their board and care. Sometimes they

133

would take it and buy me something with it. Sometimes they completely refused to take it.

Slowly, and with much support and encouragement from Linda her family, I started eating normally again and gained weight. I felt my confidence grow with each passing day. They showed me that not only was I loveable, but also that none of what happened was my fault. I began to blossom physically but there were still mental scars that affected me – feelings of inadequacy, sadness, and guilt would often sweep over me at unexpected times. I often felt immense anger towards people who had better parents than me and towards Mum and Jim for the things they did. At night time I'd wake up bathed in sweat, feeling like I was falling from a great height and nothing or no one could save me. A silent tsunami of tears would fall, choking me with sobs so hard I thought I would drown from it all. I tried to put these feelings into a box in my mind and lock the key. Surely if I kept them hidden, they wouldn't affect me anymore. The courage and resilience of youth was on my side. If I didn't think about what had happened to me, I knew I could heal and grow. I didn't want to feel like a victim all my life. Now I had a home and a nurturing, loving environment the possibilities were endless. I had a brand new life to start and I couldn't allow myself to feel pity for the girl I once was, or the girl I could've been if I'd grown up with a normal childhood. It had happened and there was no way to change it. I had to move on.

I passed ten GCSEs with all As and Bs and was encouraged by my teachers to stay on for two more years of sixth form, but I felt like I had to start paying my way. A local animal shelter was advertising for help so I applied and got the job. A kindly woman called Pam with ruddy cheeks and her hair in a messy bun showed me around the facility after the interview. It was heartbreaking as I watched the dogs and cats in kennels, staring at me with such an expression of sadness and hope. Immediately, a picture of my beloved Dusty came to mind, and I blinked back the tears. I empathised with these animals completely and could feel their pain. I knew what it was like to be unloved and abused with no one to rescue you. Hopefully, I could make their lives more bearable.

My duties were walking the dogs, cleaning out all the cages, and feeding the animals. Every day I'd come home from work sad to leave them there, chattering about all the dogs and cats and their different personalities, and hoping that Linda would let me bring some home to live.

'We can't have a dog when we're out all day working,' she said one day, 'but you're welcome to bring a cat home.'

I was so excited the next day when I went to work, knowing exactly which little kitten I would rehouse. She was a small, long-haired tabby that I renamed Rosemary after my Nan. I knew it was a silly name for a cat, but I wanted to honour her memory in some small way. Rosemary fitted in right away and everyone fell in love with her. In the witching hour, when my nightmares would break out of their box, Rosemary was always there, snuggled into me in bed, to give me a reassuring lick and a purr.

When I was eighteen I saw a job advertised for a receptionist at a nearby veterinary clinic and got the job. The owners were so impressed by me that they offered to promote me to a trainee veterinary nurse, learning on the job and with day releases to college. It was a dream come true.

I visited the local pubs and clubs with Beth and our friends at the weekends, drinking and dancing the night away, and met my first boyfriend called Tom. When he asked me to go out for a drink with him the following week, I was so shocked I thought he was talking to one of the other girls.

Beth helped me get ready for our date, doing my hair and makeup in the role of doting big sister that she'd assumed for the past two years. Butterflies filled my stomach as he rang the doorbell and I waited to meet him.

He had a great sense of humor, something which was so important to me. I hadn't had much laughter growing up, and now I craved it. We took things slowly for a long time as I found it hard to trust people. It took me months to pluck up the courage to tell him what had happened in the past, fearing that he would either blame me or see me through Mum and Jim's eyes as unlovable. He comforted me through my tears, telling me how brave I was and how strong I'd become. He'd had no idea about my past. The child that I kept locked in that box in my mind with the darkest memories was hidden from the surface. If you took one look at me, you'd see an outgoing, confident, happy young woman. Probe deeper, and you'd see the hint of fragileness, insecurity, and fear that would pop up from under the surface now and again to rear its ugly head. But he never seemed to notice the old me. In his eyes, he only saw the new me. He was horrified about what Mum and Jim had put me through, and when the witching hour came around, he was the one to comfort me now, constantly reassuring me and telling me everything would be OK. He became my rock, and the first time we slept with each other, I knew I was in love with him. I was worried about him seeing the ugly cigarette burns and scars, but as I nervously undressed, he kissed each one of them gently before telling me how perfect I was.

Just before my twentieth birthday, two amazing things happened. I passed my veterinary nurse exam, bringing with it a pay rise, and Tom proposed to me. Linda, Clive, Beth, and Jane held a family party to celebrate, with Linda cooking up a storm in the kitchen all day and me helping her make the cake.

After she'd mixed up all the cake mixture and poured it into the baking tin she handed me the bowl. 'Do you want to lick the mixture? I remember how you always used to love doing that.'

I don't know if it was the way she looked at me with such love, or the reminder that it's what Nan always let me do when she was cooking her fairy cakes, or the emotion of getting engaged, but suddenly the tears streamed down my face.

I'd been to hell and back, coming a full circle, but now I was finally home. My whole life stretched ahead of me, filled with possibilities. I had survived.

# EPILOGUE

Whilst it was Linda and Clive who saved my life, Tom continues to save it every day. I will always be eternally grateful to him, Linda, Clive, Beth and Jane, and without them, I would not be where I am today. Tom and I are still married and we have a son and daughter of our own now. He's not just the love of my life – he is my family. Five years ago, we opened my own cattery, and have numerous rescue animals. I would like to thank all of my family for healing my wounds and filling me with love and happiness.

This book was very hard to write, but I think it was very therapeutic for me to get it all out of my head and onto the pages. I debated about what to include, having forgotten a lot of things or hidden the horrors away in my memory, but in the end I wanted you to know the events that had the most effect on my life.

In my early twenties I sought counselling. I wanted to try and understand how a mother can treat their child with such cruelty. I tried one counsellor but I never felt very comfortable, and their opinion was that I had to forgive Mum to be able to move on. At that time I wasn't ready to forgive her. I don't think I ever will be, and after a month of having achieved very little, I never went back. What did help me immensely was the love of my husband, my new family, and a healer I met about three years ago. With the power of positive mantras and affirmations, I learnt to forgive myself for feeling unworthy of love and let go of my final ghosts of the child that was Sarah.

Looking back now, I realise that Mum suffered from postnatal depression when she had me. The death of my dad before she'd full recovered obviously knocked her down further. I think this then developed into manic-depression, what would these days be called bipolar disorder. Back then there was inadequate care in the community to monitor patients with psychiatric problems, and she often refused to take her medication. I do wonder whether she would have acted differently towards me if she had been medically treated properly but that's a question that I can never find an answer to, and one that I've learnt over the years to avoid asking myself.

Do I feel let down by the system? Absolutely. I had numerous hospital visits over the years to treat injuries with no questions asked. Often, I was black and blue when I arrived at school. How could the doctors and teachers not notice that and think something was seriously wrong? No one lifted a finger to end my suffering.

I never wanted to have anything more to do with Mum after I left home at fifteen, but I did want to keep in touch with Kaley. I never knew where they went when they left the village. When my daughter was born, I had an inexplicable desire to try and find Mum again. I needed to know why she'd done the things she had and whether she'd changed, but I never found out where they were, and maybe that's for the best. I hope my sister is living a fantastic life and I would love to meet her.

I wrote this book hoping that it would make others more aware of what an abused child looks like so they can take some positive action to help them. The child who goes to school smelling of urine, the one with the dirty hair and unkempt look, the one who isn't allowed to play with her friends, the one who steals food because she's not being fed properly, the one who is lonely and isolated, the one who has bruises and cuts that can't be explained constantly by being 'clumsy.' That's a child people need to look more closely at.

Mum did teach me one lesson in life, and it's a valuable one that I make sure I practice every day. She taught me how NOT to be a mother like her. She taught me how NOT to treat my children like her. In her own way, she made me who I am today: A strong, confident woman and a loving mother and wife who wears a happy smile.

One of the positive mantras that I still repeat on a daily basis is, 'You can achieve anything you want.' I believe the substance and wording of this mantra really is true. I have achieved the happy and loving life I strived for all those years ago, although it hasn't been easy, and there have been many struggles along the way, but I did it. So I'd like to leave you with one final thought…

If I can do anything I want, then so can you. It

takes a lot of little steps to climb a mountain, but I made it, and the view from here is great!

Made in the USA
Columbia, SC
29 May 2020

98645075R00088